DIRECTORY

NAME	ADDRESS		NE

5784 2024	**August**		tamuz av
SUNDAY	**MONDAY**	**TUESDAY**	**WEDNESDAY**
4 29 tamuz	**5** 1 av ROSH CHODESH	**6** 2 av	**7** 3 av
11 7 av	**12** 8 av EREV TISHA B'AV	**13** 9 av TISHA B'AV	**14** 10 av
18 14 av	**19** 15 av TU B'AV	**20** 16 av	**21** 17 av
25 21 av	**26** 22 av	**27** 23 av	**28** 24 av

THURSDAY	FRIDAY	SATURDAY
1 26 tamuz	**2** 27 tamuz	**3** 28 tamuz *Matot-Masei*
8 4 av	**9** 5 av	**10** 6 av *Devarim* **SHABBAT CHAZON**
15 11 av	**16** 12 av	**17** 13 av *Ve'etchanan* **SHABBAT NACHAMU**
22 18 av	**23** 19 av	**24** 20 av *Eikev*
29 25 av	**30** 26 av	**31** 27 av *Re'eh*

5785

SEPTEMBER
S	M	T	W	T	F	S
1	2	3	4	5	6	7
8	9	10	11	12	13	14
15	16	17	18	19	20	21
22	23	24	25	26	27	28
29	30					

OCTOBER
S	M	T	W	T	F	S
		1	2	3	4	5
6	7	8	9	10	11	12
13	14	15	16	17	18	19
20	21	22	23	24	25	26
27	28	29	30	31		

NOVEMBER
S	M	T	W	T	F	S
					1	2
3	4	5	6	7	8	9
10	11	12	13	14	15	16
17	18	19	20	21	22	23
24	25	26	27	28	29	30

DECEMBER
S	M	T	W	T	F	S
1	2	3	4	5	6	7
8	9	10	11	12	13	14
15	16	17	18	19	20	21
22	23	24	25	26	27	28
29	30	31				

JANUARY
S	M	T	W	T	F	S
			1	2	3	4
5	6	7	8	9	10	11
12	13	14	15	16	17	18
19	20	21	22	23	24	25
26	27	28	29	30	31	

FEBRUARY
S	M	T	W	T	F	S
						1
2	3	4	5	6	7	8
9	10	11	12	13	14	15
16	17	18	19	20	21	22
23	24	25	26	27	28	

MARCH
S	M	T	W	T	F	S
						1
2	3	4	5	6	7	8
9	10	11	12	13	14	15
16	17	18	19	20	21	22
23 30	24 31	25	26	27	28	29

APRIL
S	M	T	W	T	F	S
		1	2	3	4	5
6	7	8	9	10	11	12
13	14	15	16	17	18	19
20	21	22	23	24	25	26
27	28	29	30			

MAY
S	M	T	W	T	F	S
				1	2	3
4	5	6	7	8	9	10
11	12	13	14	15	16	17
18	19	20	21	22	23	24
25	26	27	28	29	30	31

JUNE
S	M	T	W	T	F	S
1	2	3	4	5	6	7
8	9	10	11	12	13	14
15	16	17	18	19	20	21
22	23	24	25	26	27	28
29	30					

JULY
S	M	T	W	T	F	S
		1	2	3	4	5
6	7	8	9	10	11	12
13	14	15	16	17	18	19
20	21	22	23	24	25	26
27	28	29	30	31		

AUGUST
S	M	T	W	T	F	S
					1	2
3	4	5	6	7	8	9
10	11	12	13	14	15	16
17	18	19	20	21	22	23
24 31	25	26	27	28	29	30

September

5784
2024

SUNDAY	MONDAY	TUESDAY	WEDNESDAY
1 28 av	**2** 29 av LABOR DAY	**3** 30 av **ROSH CHODESH**	**4** 1 elul **ROSH CHODESH**
8 5 elul	**9** 6 elul	**10** 7 elul	**11** 8 elul
15 12 elul	**16** 13 elul	**17** 14 elul	**18** 15 elul
22 19 elul FALL BEGINS	**23** 20 elul	**24** 21 elul	**25** 22 elul
29 26 elul	**30** 27 elul		

av
elul

THURSDAY	FRIDAY	SATURDAY
5 — 2 elul	**6** — 3 elul	**7** — 4 elul *Shoftim*
12 — 9 elul	**13** — 10 elul	**14** — 11 elul *Ki Teitzei*
19 — 16 elul	**20** — 17 elul	**21** — 18 elul *Ki Tavo*
26 — 23 elul	**27** — 24 elul	**28** — 25 elul *Nitzavim-Vayeilech* **SELICHOT**

5785

SEPTEMBER
S	M	T	W	T	F	S
1	2	3	4	5	6	7
8	9	10	11	12	13	14
15	16	17	18	19	20	21
22	23	24	25	26	27	28
29	30					

OCTOBER
S	M	T	W	T	F	S
		1	2	3	4	5
6	7	8	9	10	11	12
13	14	15	16	17	18	19
20	21	22	23	24	25	26
27	28	29	30	31		

NOVEMBER
S	M	T	W	T	F	S
					1	2
3	4	5	6	7	8	9
10	11	12	13	14	15	16
17	18	19	20	21	22	23
24	25	26	27	28	29	30

DECEMBER
S	M	T	W	T	F	S
1	2	3	4	5	6	7
8	9	10	11	12	13	14
15	16	17	18	19	20	21
22	23	24	25	26	27	28
29	30	31				

JANUARY
S	M	T	W	T	F	S
			1	2	3	4
5	6	7	8	9	10	11
12	13	14	15	16	17	18
19	20	21	22	23	24	25
26	27	28	29	30	31	

FEBRUARY
S	M	T	W	T	F	S
						1
2	3	4	5	6	7	8
9	10	11	12	13	14	15
16	17	18	19	20	21	22
23	24	25	26	27	28	

MARCH
S	M	T	W	T	F	S
						1
2	3	4	5	6	7	8
9	10	11	12	13	14	15
16	17	18	19	20	21	22
23 30	24 31	25	26	27	28	29

APRIL
S	M	T	W	T	F	S
		1	2	3	4	5
6	7	8	9	10	11	12
13	14	15	16	17	18	19
20	21	22	23	24	25	26
27	28	29	30			

MAY
S	M	T	W	T	F	S
				1	2	3
4	5	6	7	8	9	10
11	12	13	14	15	16	17
18	19	20	21	22	23	24
25	26	27	28	29	30	31

JUNE
S	M	T	W	T	F	S
1	2	3	4	5	6	7
8	9	10	11	12	13	14
15	16	17	18	19	20	21
22	23	24	25	26	27	28
29	30					

JULY
S	M	T	W	T	F	S
		1	2	3	4	5
6	7	8	9	10	11	12
13	14	15	16	17	18	19
20	21	22	23	24	25	26
27	28	29	30	31		

AUGUST
S	M	T	W	T	F	S
					1	2
3	4	5	6	7	8	9
10	11	12	13	14	15	16
17	18	19	20	21	22	23
24 31	25	26	27	28	29	30

October

5784–85
2024

elul
tishri

SUNDAY	MONDAY	TUESDAY	WEDNESDAY
		1 28 elul	**2** 29 elul **EREV ROSH HASHANAH**
6 4 tishri **FAST OF GEDALIAH**	**7** 5 tishri	**8** 6 tishri	**9** 7 tishri
13 11 tishri	**14** 12 tishri CANADIAN THANKSGIVING COLUMBUS DAY INDIGENOUS PEOPLES DAY	**15** 13 tishri	**16** 14 tishri **EREV SUKKOT**
20 18 tishri **INTERMEDIATE DAY**	**21** 19 tishri **INTERMEDIATE DAY**	**22** 20 tishri **INTERMEDIATE DAY**	**23** 21 tishri **HOSHANAH RABBAH**
27 25 tishri	**28** 26 tishri	**29** 27 tishri	**30** 28 tishri

NOTES:

THURSDAY	FRIDAY	SATURDAY
3 1 tishri	**4** 2 tishri	**5** 3 tishri *Ha'azinu*
ROSH HASHANAH	ROSH HASHANAH	SHABBAT SHUVAH
10 8 tishri	**11** 9 tishri	**12** 10 tishri
	KOL NIDRE	YIZKOR YOM KIPPUR
17 15 tishri	**18** 16 tishri	**19** 17 tishri
SUKKOT	SUKKOT	INTERMEDIATE DAY
24 22 tishri	**25** 23 tishri	**26** 24 tishri
YIZKOR SHEMINI ATZERET	SIMCHAT TORAH	*Breshit*
31 29 tishri		

5785

SEPTEMBER
S M T W T F S
1 2 3 4 5 6 7
8 9 10 11 12 13 14
15 16 17 18 19 20 21
22 23 24 25 26 27 28
29 30

OCTOBER
S M T W T F S
1 2 3 4 5
6 7 8 9 10 11 12
13 14 15 16 17 18 19
20 21 22 23 24 25 26
27 28 29 30 31

NOVEMBER
S M T W T F S
1 2
3 4 5 6 7 8 9
10 11 12 13 14 15 16
17 18 19 20 21 22 23
24 25 26 27 28 29 30

DECEMBER
S M T W T F S
1 2 3 4 5 6 7
8 9 10 11 12 13 14
15 16 17 18 19 20 21
22 23 24 25 26 27 28
29 30 31

JANUARY
S M T W T F S
1 2 3 4
5 6 7 8 9 10 11
12 13 14 15 16 17 18
19 20 21 22 23 24 25
26 27 28 29 30 31

FEBRUARY
S M T W T F S
1
2 3 4 5 6 7 8
9 10 11 12 13 14 15
16 17 18 19 20 21 22
23 24 25 26 27 28

MARCH
S M T W T F S
1
2 3 4 5 6 7 8
9 10 11 12 13 14 15
16 17 18 19 20 21 22
23 30 24 31 25 26 27 28 29

APRIL
S M T W T F S
1 2 3 4 5
6 7 8 9 10 11 12
13 14 15 16 17 18 19
20 21 22 23 24 25 26
27 28 29 30

MAY
S M T W T F S
1 2 3
4 5 6 7 8 9 10
11 12 13 14 15 16 17
18 19 20 21 22 23 24
25 26 27 28 29 30 31

JUNE
S M T W T F S
1 2 3 4 5 6 7
8 9 10 11 12 13 14
15 16 17 18 19 20 21
22 23 24 25 26 27 28
29 30

JULY
S M T W T F S
1 2 3 4 5
6 7 8 9 10 11 12
13 14 15 16 17 18 19
20 21 22 23 24 25 26
27 28 29 30 31

AUGUST
S M T W T F S
1 2
3 4 5 6 7 8 9
10 11 12 13 14 15 16
17 18 19 20 21 22 23
24 31 25 26 27 28 29 30

5785 2024 November

SUNDAY	MONDAY	TUESDAY	WEDNESDAY
3 2 cheshvan	**4** 3 cheshvan	**5** 4 cheshvan	**6** 5 cheshvan
10 9 cheshvan	**11** 10 cheshvan CANADIAN REMEMBERANCE DAY VETERANS DAY	**12** 11 cheshvan	**13** 12 cheshvan
17 16 cheshvan	**18** 17 cheshvan	**19** 18 cheshvan	**20** 19 cheshvan
24 23 cheshvan	**25** 24 cheshvan	**26** 25 cheshvan	**27** 26 cheshvan

tishri
cheshvan

THURSDAY	FRIDAY	SATURDAY
	1 30 tishri 🕯️ **ROSH CHODESH**	**2** 1 cheshvan 📜 *Noach* **ROSH CHODESH**
7 6 cheshvan	**8** 7 cheshvan 🕯️	**9** 8 cheshvan 📜 *Lech Lecha*
14 13 cheshvan	**15** 14 cheshvan 🕯️	**16** 15 cheshvan 📜 *Vayera*
21 20 cheshvan	**22** 21 cheshvan 🕯️	**23** 22 cheshvan 📜 *Chaye Sarah*
28 27 cheshvan THANKSGIVING	**29** 28 cheshvan 🕯️	**30** 29 cheshvan 📜 *Toldot* SIGD

5785

SEPTEMBER						
S	M	T	W	T	F	S
1	2	3	4	5	6	7
8	9	10	11	12	13	14
15	16	17	18	19	20	21
22	23	24	25	26	27	28
29	30					

OCTOBER						
S	M	T	W	T	F	S
		1	2	3	4	5
6	7	8	9	10	11	12
13	14	15	16	17	18	19
20	21	22	23	24	25	26
27	28	29	30	31		

NOVEMBER						
S	M	T	W	T	F	S
					1	2
3	4	5	6	7	8	9
10	11	12	13	14	15	16
17	18	19	20	21	22	23
24	25	26	27	28	29	30

DECEMBER						
S	M	T	W	T	F	S
1	2	3	4	5	6	7
8	9	10	11	12	13	14
15	16	17	18	19	20	21
22	23	24	25	26	27	28
29	30	31				

JANUARY						
S	M	T	W	T	F	S
			1	2	3	4
5	6	7	8	9	10	11
12	13	14	15	16	17	18
19	20	21	22	23	24	25
26	27	28	29	30	31	

FEBRUARY						
S	M	T	W	T	F	S
						1
2	3	4	5	6	7	8
9	10	11	12	13	14	15
16	17	18	19	20	21	22
23	24	25	26	27	28	

MARCH						
S	M	T	W	T	F	S
						1
2	3	4	5	6	7	8
9	10	11	12	13	14	15
16	17	18	19	20	21	22
23 30	24 31	25	26	27	28	29

APRIL						
S	M	T	W	T	F	S
		1	2	3	4	5
6	7	8	9	10	11	12
13	14	15	16	17	18	19
20	21	22	23	24	25	26
27	28	29	30			

MAY						
S	M	T	W	T	F	S
				1	2	3
4	5	6	7	8	9	10
11	12	13	14	15	16	17
18	19	20	21	22	23	24
25	26	27	28	29	30	31

JUNE						
S	M	T	W	T	F	S
1	2	3	4	5	6	7
8	9	10	11	12	13	14
15	16	17	18	19	20	21
22	23	24	25	26	27	28
29	30					

JULY						
S	M	T	W	T	F	S
		1	2	3	4	5
6	7	8	9	10	11	12
13	14	15	16	17	18	19
20	21	22	23	24	25	26
27	28	29	30	31		

AUGUST						
S	M	T	W	T	F	S
					1	2
3	4	5	6	7	8	9
10	11	12	13	14	15	16
17	18	19	20	21	22	23
24 31	25	26	27	28	29	30

5785
2024
December

SUNDAY	MONDAY	TUESDAY	WEDNESDAY
1 30 cheshvan **ROSH CHODESH**	**2** 1 kislev **ROSH CHODESH**	**3** 2 kislev	**4** 3 kislev
8 7 kislev	**9** 8 kislev	**10** 9 kislev	**11** 10 kislev
15 14 kislev	**16** 15 kislev	**17** 16 kislev	**18** 17 kislev
22 21 kislev	**23** 22 kislev	**24** 23 kislev	**25** 24 kislev CHRISTMAS DAY **EREV HANUKKAH**
29 28 kislev **HANUKKAH**	**30** 29 kislev **HANUKKAH**	**31** 30 kislev **ROSH CHODESH** **HANUKKAH**	

cheshvan
kislev

THURSDAY	FRIDAY	SATURDAY
5 — 4 kislev	**6** — 5 kislev	**7** — 6 kislev *Vayetzei*
12 — 11 kislev	**13** — 12 kislev	**14** — 13 kislev *Vayishlach*
19 — 18 kislev	**20** — 19 kislev	**21** — 20 kislev *Vayeshev*
26 — 25 kislev HANUKKAH	**27** — 26 kislev HANUKKAH	**28** — 27 kislev *Miketz* HANUKKAH

5785

SEPTEMBER								OCTOBER						
S	M	T	W	T	F	S		S	M	T	W	T	F	S
1	2	3	4	5	6	7				1	2	3	4	5
8	9	10	11	12	13	14		6	7	8	9	10	11	12
15	16	17	18	19	20	21		13	14	15	16	17	18	19
22	23	24	25	26	27	28		20	21	22	23	24	25	26
29	30							27	28	29	30	31		

NOVEMBER								DECEMBER						
S	M	T	W	T	F	S		S	M	T	W	T	F	S
					1	2		1	2	3	4	5	6	7
3	4	5	6	7	8	9		8	9	10	11	12	13	14
10	11	12	13	14	15	16		15	16	17	18	19	20	21
17	18	19	20	21	22	23		22	23	24	25	26	27	28
24	25	26	27	28	29	30		29	30	31				

JANUARY								FEBRUARY						
S	M	T	W	T	F	S		S	M	T	W	T	F	S
			1	2	3	4								1
5	6	7	8	9	10	11		2	3	4	5	6	7	8
12	13	14	15	16	17	18		9	10	11	12	13	14	15
19	20	21	22	23	24	25		16	17	18	19	20	21	22
26	27	28	29	30	31			23	24	25	26	27	28	

MARCH								APRIL						
S	M	T	W	T	F	S		S	M	T	W	T	F	S
						1				1	2	3	4	5
2	3	4	5	6	7	8		6	7	8	9	10	11	12
9	10	11	12	13	14	15		13	14	15	16	17	18	19
16	17	18	19	20	21	22		20	21	22	23	24	25	26
23₃₀	24₃₁	25	26	27	28	29		27	28	29	30			

MAY								JUNE						
S	M	T	W	T	F	S		S	M	T	W	T	F	S
				1	2	3		1	2	3	4	5	6	7
4	5	6	7	8	9	10		8	9	10	11	12	13	14
11	12	13	14	15	16	17		15	16	17	18	19	20	21
18	19	20	21	22	23	24		22	23	24	25	26	27	28
25	26	27	28	29	30	31		29	30					

JULY								AUGUST						
S	M	T	W	T	F	S		S	M	T	W	T	F	S
		1	2	3	4	5							1	2
6	7	8	9	10	11	12		3	4	5	6	7	8	9
13	14	15	16	17	18	19		10	11	12	13	14	15	16
20	21	22	23	24	25	26		17	18	19	20	21	22	23
27	28	29	30	31				24₃₁	25	26	27	28	29	30

5785 / 2025

January

tevet shevat

SUNDAY	MONDAY	TUESDAY	WEDNESDAY
			1 — 1 tevet NEW YEAR'S DAY **ROSH CHODESH** **HANUKKAH**
5 — 5 tevet	**6** — 6 tevet	**7** — 7 tevet	**8** — 8 tevet
12 — 12 tevet	**13** — 13 tevet	**14** — 14 tevet	**15** — 15 tevet
19 — 19 tevet	**20** — 20 tevet MARTIN LUTHER KING DAY	**21** — 21 tevet	**22** — 22 tevet
26 — 26 tevet	**27** — 27 tevet	**28** — 28 tevet	**29** — 29 tevet

THURSDAY	FRIDAY	SATURDAY
2 2 tevet	**3** 3 tevet	**4** 4 tevet
HANUKKAH		*Vayigash*
9 9 tevet	**10** 10 tevet	**11** 11 tevet
	FAST OF 10TH OF TEVET	*Vayechi*
16 16 tevet	**17** 17 tevet	**18** 18 tevet
		Shemot
23 23 tevet	**24** 24 tevet	**25** 25 tevet
		Vaera
30 1 shevat	**31** 2 shevat	
ROSH CHODESH		

5785

SEPTEMBER
S	M	T	W	T	F	S
1	2	3	4	5	6	7
8	9	10	11	12	13	14
15	16	17	18	19	20	21
22	23	24	25	26	27	28
29	30					

OCTOBER
S	M	T	W	T	F	S
		1	2	3	4	5
6	7	8	9	10	11	12
13	14	15	16	17	18	19
20	21	22	23	24	25	26
27	28	29	30	31		

NOVEMBER
S	M	T	W	T	F	S
					1	2
3	4	5	6	7	8	9
10	11	12	13	14	15	16
17	18	19	20	21	22	23
24	25	26	27	28	29	30

DECEMBER
S	M	T	W	T	F	S
1	2	3	4	5	6	7
8	9	10	11	12	13	14
15	16	17	18	19	20	21
22	23	24	25	26	27	28
29	30	31				

JANUARY
S	M	T	W	T	F	S
			1	2	3	4
5	6	7	8	9	10	11
12	13	14	15	16	17	18
19	20	21	22	23	24	25
26	27	28	29	30	31	

FEBRUARY
S	M	T	W	T	F	S
						1
2	3	4	5	6	7	8
9	10	11	12	13	14	15
16	17	18	19	20	21	22
23	24	25	26	27	28	

MARCH
S	M	T	W	T	F	S
						1
2	3	4	5	6	7	8
9	10	11	12	13	14	15
16	17	18	19	20	21	22
23 30	24 31	25	26	27	28	29

APRIL
S	M	T	W	T	F	S
		1	2	3	4	5
6	7	8	9	10	11	12
13	14	15	16	17	18	19
20	21	22	23	24	25	26
27	28	29	30			

MAY
S	M	T	W	T	F	S
				1	2	3
4	5	6	7	8	9	10
11	12	13	14	15	16	17
18	19	20	21	22	23	24
25	26	27	28	29	30	31

JUNE
S	M	T	W	T	F	S
1	2	3	4	5	6	7
8	9	10	11	12	13	14
15	16	17	18	19	20	21
22	23	24	25	26	27	28
29	30					

JULY
S	M	T	W	T	F	S
		1	2	3	4	5
6	7	8	9	10	11	12
13	14	15	16	17	18	19
20	21	22	23	24	25	26
27	28	29	30	31		

AUGUST
S	M	T	W	T	F	S
					1	2
3	4	5	6	7	8	9
10	11	12	13	14	15	16
17	18	19	20	21	22	23
24 31	25	26	27	28	29	30

February

5785
2025

shevat

SUNDAY	MONDAY	TUESDAY	WEDNESDAY
2 4 shevat	3 5 shevat	4 6 shevat	5 7 shevat
9 11 shevat	10 12 shevat	11 13 shevat	12 14 shevat
16 18 shevat	17 19 shevat PRESIDENTS DAY	18 20 shevat	19 21 shevat
23 25 shevat	24 26 shevat	25 27 shevat	26 28 shevat

THURSDAY	FRIDAY	SATURDAY
		1 3 shevat *Bo*
6 8 shevat	**7** 9 shevat	**8** 10 shevat *Beshalach* **SHABBAT SHIRAH**
13 15 shevat **TU B'SHEVAT**	**14** 16 shevat	**15** 17 shevat *Yitro*
20 22 shevat	**21** 23 shevat	**22** 24 shevat *Mishpatim*
27 29 shevat	**28** 30 shevat **ROSH CHODESH**	

5785

SEPTEMBER						
S	M	T	W	T	F	S
1	2	3	4	5	6	7
8	9	10	11	12	13	14
15	16	17	18	19	20	21
22	23	24	25	26	27	28
29	30					

OCTOBER						
S	M	T	W	T	F	S
		1	2	3	4	5
6	7	8	9	10	11	12
13	14	15	16	17	18	19
20	21	22	23	24	25	26
27	28	29	30	31		

NOVEMBER						
S	M	T	W	T	F	S
					1	2
3	4	5	6	7	8	9
10	11	12	13	14	15	16
17	18	19	20	21	22	23
24	25	26	27	28	29	30

DECEMBER						
S	M	T	W	T	F	S
1	2	3	4	5	6	7
8	9	10	11	12	13	14
15	16	17	18	19	20	21
22	23	24	25	26	27	28
29	30	31				

JANUARY						
S	M	T	W	T	F	S
			1	2	3	4
5	6	7	8	9	10	11
12	13	14	15	16	17	18
19	20	21	22	23	24	25
26	27	28	29	30	31	

FEBRUARY						
S	M	T	W	T	F	S
						1
2	3	4	5	6	7	8
9	10	11	12	13	14	15
16	17	18	19	20	21	22
23	24	25	26	27	28	

MARCH						
S	M	T	W	T	F	S
						1
2	3	4	5	6	7	8
9	10	11	12	13	14	15
16	17	18	19	20	21	22
23,30	24,31	25	26	27	28	29

APRIL						
S	M	T	W	T	F	S
		1	2	3	4	5
6	7	8	9	10	11	12
13	14	15	16	17	18	19
20	21	22	23	24	25	26
27	28	29	30			

MAY						
S	M	T	W	T	F	S
				1	2	3
4	5	6	7	8	9	10
11	12	13	14	15	16	17
18	19	20	21	22	23	24
25	26	27	28	29	30	31

JUNE						
S	M	T	W	T	F	S
1	2	3	4	5	6	7
8	9	10	11	12	13	14
15	16	17	18	19	20	21
22	23	24	25	26	27	28
29	30					

JULY						
S	M	T	W	T	F	S
		1	2	3	4	5
6	7	8	9	10	11	12
13	14	15	16	17	18	19
20	21	22	23	24	25	26
27	28	29	30	31		

AUGUST						
S	M	T	W	T	F	S
					1	2
3	4	5	6	7	8	9
10	11	12	13	14	15	16
17	18	19	20	21	22	23
24,31	25	26	27	28	29	30

5785 2025   March   adar nisan

SUNDAY	MONDAY	TUESDAY	WEDNESDAY
2 2 adar	3 3 adar	4 4 adar	5 5 adar
9 9 adar	10 10 adar	11 11 adar	12 12 adar
16 16 adar	17 17 adar	18 18 adar	19 19 adar
23 23 adar	24 24 adar	25 25 adar	26 26 adar
30 1 nisan **ROSH CHODESH**	31 2 nisan		

THURSDAY	FRIDAY	SATURDAY
		1 — 1 adar *Terumah* **SHABBAT SHEKALIM** **ROSH CHODESH**
6 — 6 adar	**7** — 7 adar	**8** — 8 adar *Tetzaveh* **SHABBAT ZACHOR**
13 — 13 adar **FAST OF ESTHER**	**14** — 14 adar **PURIM**	**15** — 15 adar *Ki Tisa* **SHUSHAN PURIM**
20 — 20 adar	**21** — 21 adar	**22** — 22 adar *Vayakhel* **SHABBAT PARAH**
27 — 27 adar	**28** — 28 adar	**29** — 29 adar *Pekude*

5785

SEPTEMBER							OCTOBER						
S	M	T	W	T	F	S	S	M	T	W	T	F	S
1	2	3	4	5	6	7			1	2	3	4	5
8	9	10	11	12	13	14	6	7	8	9	10	11	12
15	16	17	18	19	20	21	13	14	15	16	17	18	19
22	23	24	25	26	27	28	20	21	22	23	24	25	26
29	30						27	28	29	30	31		

NOVEMBER							DECEMBER						
S	M	T	W	T	F	S	S	M	T	W	T	F	S
					1	2	1	2	3	4	5	6	7
3	4	5	6	7	8	9	8	9	10	11	12	13	14
10	11	12	13	14	15	16	15	16	17	18	19	20	21
17	18	19	20	21	22	23	22	23	24	25	26	27	28
24	25	26	27	28	29	30	29	30	31				

JANUARY							FEBRUARY						
S	M	T	W	T	F	S	S	M	T	W	T	F	S
			1	2	3	4							1
5	6	7	8	9	10	11	2	3	4	5	6	7	8
12	13	14	15	16	17	18	9	10	11	12	13	14	15
19	20	21	22	23	24	25	16	17	18	19	20	21	22
26	27	28	29	30	31		23	24	25	26	27	28	

MARCH							APRIL						
S	M	T	W	T	F	S	S	M	T	W	T	F	S
						1			1	2	3	4	5
2	3	4	5	6	7	8	6	7	8	9	10	11	12
9	10	11	12	13	14	15	13	14	15	16	17	18	19
16	17	18	19	20	21	22	20	21	22	23	24	25	26
23 30	24 31	25	26	27	28	29	27	28	29	30			

MAY							JUNE						
S	M	T	W	T	F	S	S	M	T	W	T	F	S
				1	2	3	1	2	3	4	5	6	7
4	5	6	7	8	9	10	8	9	10	11	12	13	14
11	12	13	14	15	16	17	15	16	17	18	19	20	21
18	19	20	21	22	23	24	22	23	24	25	26	27	28
25	26	27	28	29	30	31	29	30					

JULY							AUGUST						
S	M	T	W	T	F	S	S	M	T	W	T	F	S
		1	2	3	4	5						1	2
6	7	8	9	10	11	12	3	4	5	6	7	8	9
13	14	15	16	17	18	19	10	11	12	13	14	15	16
20	21	22	23	24	25	26	17	18	19	20	21	22	23
27	28	29	30	31			24 31	25	26	27	28	29	30

5785 2025 April nisan iyar

SUNDAY	MONDAY	TUESDAY	WEDNESDAY
		1 3 nisan	**2** 4 nisan
6 8 nisan	**7** 9 nisan	**8** 10 nisan	**9** 11 nisan
13 15 nisan **PASSOVER**	**14** 16 nisan **PASSOVER**	**15** 17 nisan **INTERMEDIATE DAY**	**16** 18 nisan **INTERMEDIATE DAY**
20 22 nisan EASTER **YIZKOR** **PASSOVER**	**21** 23 nisan	**22** 24 nisan	**23** 25 nisan
27 29 nisan	**28** 30 nisan **ROSH CHODESH**	**29** 1 iyar **ROSH CHODESH**	**30** 2 iyar **YOM HAZIKARON**

THURSDAY	FRIDAY	SATURDAY
3 5 nisan	**4** 6 nisan	**5** 7 nisar *Vayikra*
10 12 nisan	**11** 13 nisan SEARCH FOR CHAMETZ	**12** 14 nisan *Tzav* SHABBAT HAGADOL FIRST SEDER
17 19 nisan INTERMEDIATE DAY	**18** 20 nisan INTERMEDIATE DAY	**19** 21 nisan PASSOVER
24 26 nisan YOM HASHOAH	**25** 27 nisan	**26** 28 nisan *Shemini*

5785

SEPTEMBER							OCTOBER						
S	M	T	W	T	F	S	S	M	T	W	T	F	S
1	2	3	4	5	6	7			1	2	3	4	5
8	9	10	11	12	13	14	6	7	8	9	10	11	12
15	16	17	18	19	20	21	13	14	15	16	17	18	19
22	23	24	25	26	27	28	20	21	22	23	24	25	26
29	30						27	28	29	30	31		

NOVEMBER							DECEMBER						
S	M	T	W	T	F	S	S	M	T	W	T	F	S
					1	2	1	2	3	4	5	6	7
3	4	5	6	7	8	9	8	9	10	11	12	13	14
10	11	12	13	14	15	16	15	16	17	18	19	20	21
17	18	19	20	21	22	23	22	23	24	25	26	27	28
24	25	26	27	28	29	30	29	30	31				

JANUARY							FEBRUARY						
S	M	T	W	T	F	S	S	M	T	W	T	F	S
			1	2	3	4							1
5	6	7	8	9	10	11	2	3	4	5	6	7	8
12	13	14	15	16	17	18	9	10	11	12	13	14	15
19	20	21	22	23	24	25	16	17	18	19	20	21	22
26	27	28	29	30	31		23	24	25	26	27	28	

MARCH							APRIL						
S	M	T	W	T	F	S	S	M	T	W	T	F	S
						1			1	2	3	4	5
2	3	4	5	6	7	8	6	7	8	9	10	11	12
9	10	11	12	13	14	15	13	14	15	16	17	18	19
16	17	18	19	20	21	22	20	21	22	23	24	25	26
23 30	24 31	25	26	27	28	29	27	28	29	30			

MAY							JUNE						
S	M	T	W	T	F	S	S	M	T	W	T	F	S
				1	2	3	1	2	3	4	5	6	7
4	5	6	7	8	9	10	8	9	10	11	12	13	14
11	12	13	14	15	16	17	15	16	17	18	19	20	21
18	19	20	21	22	23	24	22	23	24	25	26	27	28
25	26	27	28	29	30	31	29	30					

JULY							AUGUST						
S	M	T	W	T	F	S	S	M	T	W	T	F	S
		1	2	3	4	5						1	2
6	7	8	9	10	11	12	3	4	5	6	7	8	9
13	14	15	16	17	18	19	10	11	12	13	14	15	16
20	21	22	23	24	25	26	17	18	19	20	21	22	23
27	28	29	30	31			24 31	25	26	27	28	29	30

5785 2025 May iyar sivan

SUNDAY	MONDAY	TUESDAY	WEDNESDAY
4 — 6 iyar	5 — 7 iyar	6 — 8 iyar	7 — 9 iyar
11 — 13 iyar MOTHER'S DAY	12 — 14 iyar	13 — 15 iyar	14 — 16 iyar
18 — 20 iyar	19 — 21 iyar VICTORIA DAY CANADA	20 — 22 iyar	21 — 23 iyar
25 — 27 iyar	26 — 28 iyar MEMORIAL DAY	27 — 29 iyar	28 — 1 sivan ROSH CHODESH

THURSDAY	FRIDAY	SATURDAY
1 3 iyar	**2** 4 iyar	**3** 5 iyar
YOM HA'ATZMAUT		*Tazria-Metzora*
8 10 iyar	**9** 11 iyar	**10** 12 iyar
		Achrei Mot-Kedoshim
15 17 iyar	**16** 18 iyar	**17** 19 iyar
	LAG BA'OMER	*Emor*
22 24 iyar	**23** 25 iyar	**24** 26 iyar
		Behar-Bechukotai
29 2 sivan	**30** 3 sivan	**31** 4 sivan
		Bamidbar

5785

SEPTEMBER		OCTOBER	

SEPTEMBER
S M T W T F S
1 2 3 4 5 6 7
8 9 10 11 12 13 14
15 16 17 18 19 20 21
22 23 24 25 26 27 28
29 30

OCTOBER
S M T W T F S
1 2 3 4 5
6 7 8 9 10 11 12
13 14 15 16 17 18 19
20 21 22 23 24 25 26
27 28 29 30 31

NOVEMBER
S M T W T F S
1 2
3 4 5 6 7 8 9
10 11 12 13 14 15 16
17 18 19 20 21 22 23
24 25 26 27 28 29 30

DECEMBER
S M T W T F S
1 2 3 4 5 6 7
8 9 10 11 12 13 14
15 16 17 18 19 20 21
22 23 24 25 26 27 28
29 30 31

JANUARY
S M T W T F S
1 2 3 4
5 6 7 8 9 10 11
12 13 14 15 16 17 18
19 20 21 22 23 24 25
26 27 28 29 30 31

FEBRUARY
S M T W T F S
1
2 3 4 5 6 7 8
9 10 11 12 13 14 15
16 17 18 19 20 21 22
23 24 25 26 27 28

MARCH
S M T W T F S
1
2 3 4 5 6 7 8
9 10 11 12 13 14 15
16 17 18 19 20 21 22
23 30 24 31 25 26 27 28 29

APRIL
S M T W T F S
1 2 3 4 5
6 7 8 9 10 11 12
13 14 15 16 17 18 19
20 21 22 23 24 25 26
27 28 29 30

MAY
S M T W T F S
1 2 3
4 5 6 7 8 9 10
11 12 13 14 15 16 17
18 19 20 21 22 23 24
25 26 27 28 29 30 31

JUNE
S M T W T F S
1 2 3 4 5 6 7
8 9 10 11 12 13 14
15 16 17 18 19 20 21
22 23 24 25 26 27 28
29 30

JULY
S M T W T F S
1 2 3 4 5
6 7 8 9 10 11 12
13 14 15 16 17 18 19
20 21 22 23 24 25 26
27 28 29 30 31

AUGUST
S M T W T F S
1 2
3 4 5 6 7 8 9
10 11 12 13 14 15 16
17 18 19 20 21 22 23
24 31 25 26 27 28 29 30

June

5785 / 2025

sivan
tamuz

SUNDAY	MONDAY	TUESDAY	WEDNESDAY
1 — 5 sivan **EREV SHAVUOT**	**2** — 6 sivan **SHAVUOT**	**3** — 7 sivan **SHAVUOT**	**4** — 8 sivan
8 — 12 sivan	**9** — 13 sivan	**10** — 14 sivan	**11** — 15 sivan
15 — 19 sivan FATHER'S DAY	**16** — 20 sivan	**17** — 21 sivan	**18** — 22 sivan
22 — 26 sivan	**23** — 27 sivan	**24** — 28 sivan	**25** — 29 sivan
29 — 3 tamuz	**30** — 4 tamuz		

THURSDAY	FRIDAY	SATURDAY
5 — 9 sivan	**6** — 10 sivan	**7** — 11 sivan *Nasso*
12 — 16 sivan	**13** — 17 sivan	**14** — 18 sivan *Beha'alotecha* FLAG DAY
19 — 23 sivan JUNETEENTH	**20** — 24 sivan SUMMER BEGINS	**21** — 25 sivan *Sh'lach*
26 — 30 sivan **ROSH CHODESH**	**27** — 1 tamuz **ROSH CHODESH**	**28** — 2 tamuz *Korach*

5785

SEPTEMBER
S	M	T	W	T	F	S
	1	2	3	4	5	6	7
8	9	10	11	12	13	14
15	16	17	18	19	20	21
22	23	24	25	26	27	28
29	30					

OCTOBER
S	M	T	W	T	F	S
			1	2	3	4	5
6	7	8	9	10	11	12
13	14	15	16	17	18	19
20	21	22	23	24	25	26
27	28	29	30	31		

NOVEMBER
S	M	T	W	T	F	S
					1	2
3	4	5	6	7	8	9
10	11	12	13	14	15	16
17	18	19	20	21	22	23
24	25	26	27	28	29	30

DECEMBER
S	M	T	W	T	F	S
1	2	3	4	5	6	7
8	9	10	11	12	13	14
15	16	17	18	19	20	21
22	23	24	25	26	27	28
29	30	31				

JANUARY
S	M	T	W	T	F	S
			1	2	3	4
5	6	7	8	9	10	11
12	13	14	15	16	17	18
19	20	21	22	23	24	25
26	27	28	29	30	31	

FEBRUARY
S	M	T	W	T	F	S
						1
2	3	4	5	6	7	8
9	10	11	12	13	14	15
16	17	18	19	20	21	22
23	24	25	26	27	28	

MARCH
S	M	T	W	T	F	S
						1
2	3	4	5	6	7	8
9	10	11	12	13	14	15
16	17	18	19	20	21	22
23 30	24 31	25	26	27	28	29

APRIL
S	M	T	W	T	F	S
		1	2	3	4	5
6	7	8	9	10	11	12
13	14	15	16	17	18	19
20	21	22	23	24	25	26
27	28	29	30			

MAY
S	M	T	W	T	F	S
				1	2	3
4	5	6	7	8	9	10
11	12	13	14	15	16	17
18	19	20	21	22	23	24
25	26	27	28	29	30	31

JUNE
S	M	T	W	T	F	S
1	2	3	4	5	6	7
8	9	10	11	12	13	14
15	16	17	18	19	20	21
22	23	24	25	26	27	28
29	30					

JULY
S	M	T	W	T	F	S
		1	2	3	4	5
6	7	8	9	10	11	12
13	14	15	16	17	18	19
20	21	22	23	24	25	26
27	28	29	30	31		

AUGUST
S	M	T	W	T	F	S
					1	2
3	4	5	6	7	8	9
10	11	12	13	14	15	16
17	18	19	20	21	22	23
24 31	25	26	27	28	29	30

5785 2025 July — tamuz av

SUNDAY	MONDAY	TUESDAY	WEDNESDAY
		1 5 tamuz	2 6 tamuz
6 10 tamuz	7 11 tamuz	8 12 tamuz	9 13 tamuz
13 17 tamuz **FAST OF 17TH OF TAMUZ**	14 18 tamuz	15 19 tamuz	16 20 tamuz
20 24 tamuz	21 25 tamuz	22 26 tamuz	23 27 tamuz
27 2 av	28 3 av	29 4 av	30 5 av

THURSDAY	FRIDAY	SATURDAY
3 7 tamuz	**4** 8 tamuz INDEPENDENCE DAY	**5** 9 tamuz *Chukat*
10 14 tamuz	**11** 15 tamuz	**12** 16 tamuz *Balak*
17 21 tamuz	**18** 22 tamuz	**19** 23 tamuz *Pinchas*
24 28 tamuz	**25** 29 tamuz	**26** 1 av *Matot-Masei* **ROSH CHODESH**
31 6 av		

5785

SEPTEMBER
S	M	T	W	T	F	S
1	2	3	4	5	6	7
8	9	10	11	12	13	14
15	16	17	18	19	20	21
22	23	24	25	26	27	28
29	30					

OCTOBER
S	M	T	W	T	F	S
		1	2	3	4	5
6	7	8	9	10	11	12
13	14	15	16	17	18	19
20	21	22	23	24	25	26
27	28	29	30	31		

NOVEMBER
S	M	T	W	T	F	S
					1	2
3	4	5	6	7	8	9
10	11	12	13	14	15	16
17	18	19	20	21	22	23
24	25	26	27	28	29	30

DECEMBER
S	M	T	W	T	F	S
1	2	3	4	5	6	7
8	9	10	11	12	13	14
15	16	17	18	19	20	21
22	23	24	25	26	27	28
29	30	31				

JANUARY
S	M	T	W	T	F	S
			1	2	3	4
5	6	7	8	9	10	11
12	13	14	15	16	17	18
19	20	21	22	23	24	25
26	27	28	29	30	31	

FEBRUARY
S	M	T	W	T	F	S
						1
2	3	4	5	6	7	8
9	10	11	12	13	14	15
16	17	18	19	20	21	22
23	24	25	26	27	28	

MARCH
S	M	T	W	T	F	S
						1
2	3	4	5	6	7	8
9	10	11	12	13	14	15
16	17	18	19	20	21	22
23₃₀ 24₃₁	25	26	27	28	29	

APRIL
S	M	T	W	T	F	S
		1	2	3	4	5
6	7	8	9	10	11	12
13	14	15	16	17	18	19
20	21	22	23	24	25	26
27	28	29	30			

MAY
S	M	T	W	T	F	S
				1	2	3
4	5	6	7	8	9	10
11	12	13	14	15	16	17
18	19	20	21	22	23	24
25	26	27	28	29	30	31

JUNE
S	M	T	W	T	F	S
1	2	3	4	5	6	7
8	9	10	11	12	13	14
15	16	17	18	19	20	21
22	23	24	25	26	27	28
29	30					

JULY
S	M	T	W	T	F	S
		1	2	3	4	5
6	7	8	9	10	11	12
13	14	15	16	17	18	19
20	21	22	23	24	25	26
27	28	29	30	31		

AUGUST
S	M	T	W	T	F	S
					1	2
3	4	5	6	7	8	9
10	11	12	13	14	15	16
17	18	19	20	21	22	23
24₃₁	25	26	27	28	29	30

5785 2025 August av elul

SUNDAY	MONDAY	TUESDAY	WEDNESDAY
3 9 av **TISHA B'AV**	**4** 10 av	**5** 11 av	**6** 12 av
10 16 av	**11** 17 av	**12** 18 av	**13** 19 av
17 23 av	**18** 24 av	**19** 25 av	**20** 26 av
24 30 av **ROSH CHODESH**	**25** 1 elul **ROSH CHODESH**	**26** 2 elul	**27** 3 elul
31 7 elul			

THURSDAY	FRIDAY	SATURDAY
	1 7 av	**2** 8 av
		Devarim **SHABBAT CHAZON** **EREV TISHA B'AV**
7 13 av	**8** 14 av	**9** 15 av
		Ve'etchanan **TU B'AV** **SHABBAT NACHAMU**
14 20 av	**15** 21 av	**16** 22 av
		Eikev
21 27 av	**22** 28 av	**23** 29 av
		Re'eh
28 4 elul	**29** 5 elul	**30** 6 elul
		Shoftim

5785

SEPTEMBER
S	M	T	W	T	F	S
1	2	3	4	5	6	7
8	9	10	11	12	13	14
15	16	17	18	19	20	21
22	23	24	25	26	27	28
29	30					

OCTOBER
S	M	T	W	T	F	S
		1	2	3	4	5
6	7	8	9	10	11	12
13	14	15	16	17	18	19
20	21	22	23	24	25	26
27	28	29	30	31		

NOVEMBER
S	M	T	W	T	F	S
					1	2
3	4	5	6	7	8	9
10	11	12	13	14	15	16
17	18	19	20	21	22	23
24	25	26	27	28	29	30

DECEMBER
S	M	T	W	T	F	S
1	2	3	4	5	6	7
8	9	10	11	12	13	14
15	16	17	18	19	20	21
22	23	24	25	26	27	28
29	30	31				

JANUARY
S	M	T	W	T	F	S
			1	2	3	4
5	6	7	8	9	10	11
12	13	14	15	16	17	18
19	20	21	22	23	24	25
26	27	28	29	30	31	

FEBRUARY
S	M	T	W	T	F	S
						1
2	3	4	5	6	7	8
9	10	11	12	13	14	15
16	17	18	19	20	21	22
23	24	25	26	27	28	

MARCH
S	M	T	W	T	F	S
						1
2	3	4	5	6	7	8
9	10	11	12	13	14	15
16	17	18	19	20	21	22
23/30	24/31	25	26	27	28	29

APRIL
S	M	T	W	T	F	S
		1	2	3	4	5
6	7	8	9	10	11	12
13	14	15	16	17	18	19
20	21	22	23	24	25	26
27	28	29	30			

MAY
S	M	T	W	T	F	S
				1	2	3
4	5	6	7	8	9	10
11	12	13	14	15	16	17
18	19	20	21	22	23	24
25	26	27	28	29	30	31

JUNE
S	M	T	W	T	F	S
1	2	3	4	5	6	7
8	9	10	11	12	13	14
15	16	17	18	19	20	21
22	23	24	25	26	27	28
29	30					

JULY
S	M	T	W	T	F	S
		1	2	3	4	5
6	7	8	9	10	11	12
13	14	15	16	17	18	19
20	21	22	23	24	25	26
27	28	29	30	31		

AUGUST
S	M	T	W	T	F	S
					1	2
3	4	5	6	7	8	9
10	11	12	13	14	15	16
17	18	19	20	21	22	23
24/31	25	26	27	28	29	30

5785-86
2025

September

SUNDAY	MONDAY	TUESDAY	WEDNESDAY
	1 8 elul LABOR DAY	**2** 9 elul	**3** 10 elul
7 14 elul	**8** 15 elul	**9** 16 elul	**10** 17 elul
14 21 elul	**15** 22 elul	**16** 23 elul	**17** 24 elul
21 28 elul FALL BEGINS	**22** 29 elul 🕯 **EREV ROSH HASHANAH**	**23** 1 tishri 🕯 **ROSH HASHANAH**	**24** 2 tishri **ROSH HASHANAH**
28 6 tishri	**29** 7 tishri	**30** 8 tishri	

elul
tishri

THURSDAY	FRIDAY	SATURDAY
4 11 elul	**5** 12 elul	**6** 13 elul *Ki Teitze*
11 18 elul	**12** 19 elul	**13** 20 elul *Ki Tavo* **SELICHOT**
18 25 elul	**19** 26 elul	**20** 27 elul *Nitzavim*
25 3 tishri **FAST OF GEDALIAH**	**26** 4 tishri	**27** 5 tishri *Vayeilech* **SHABBAT SHUVAH**

5785

SEPTEMBER							OCTOBER						
S	M	T	W	T	F	S	S	M	T	W	T	F	S
1	2	3	4	5	6	7			1	2	3	4	5
8	9	10	11	12	13	14	6	7	8	9	10	11	12
15	16	17	18	19	20	21	13	14	15	16	17	18	19
22	23	24	25	26	27	28	20	21	22	23	24	25	26
29	30						27	28	29	30	31		

NOVEMBER							DECEMBER						
S	M	T	W	T	F	S	S	M	T	W	T	F	S
					1	2	1	2	3	4	5	6	7
3	4	5	6	7	8	9	8	9	10	11	12	13	14
10	11	12	13	14	15	16	15	16	17	18	19	20	21
17	18	19	20	21	22	23	22	23	24	25	26	27	28
24	25	26	27	28	29	30	29	30	31				

JANUARY							FEBRUARY						
S	M	T	W	T	F	S	S	M	T	W	T	F	S
			1	2	3	4							1
5	6	7	8	9	10	11	2	3	4	5	6	7	8
12	13	14	15	16	17	18	9	10	11	12	13	14	15
19	20	21	22	23	24	25	16	17	18	19	20	21	22
26	27	28	29	30	31		23	24	25	26	27	28	

MARCH							APRIL						
S	M	T	W	T	F	S	S	M	T	W	T	F	S
						1			1	2	3	4	5
2	3	4	5	6	7	8	6	7	8	9	10	11	12
9	10	11	12	13	14	15	13	14	15	16	17	18	19
16	17	18	19	20	21	22	20	21	22	23	24	25	26
23 30	24 31	25	26	27	28	29	27	28	29	30			

MAY							JUNE						
S	M	T	W	T	F	S	S	M	T	W	T	F	S
				1	2	3	1	2	3	4	5	6	7
4	5	6	7	8	9	10	8	9	10	11	12	13	14
11	12	13	14	15	16	17	15	16	17	18	19	20	21
18	19	20	21	22	23	24	22	23	24	25	26	27	28
25	26	27	28	29	30	31	29	30					

JULY							AUGUST						
S	M	T	W	T	F	S	S	M	T	W	T	F	S
		1	2	3	4	5						1	2
6	7	8	9	10	11	12	3	4	5	6	7	8	9
13	14	15	16	17	18	19	10	11	12	13	14	15	16
20	21	22	23	24	25	26	17	18	19	20	21	22	23
27	28	29	30	31			24 31	25	26	27	28	29	30

October

5786
2025

tishri
cheshvan

SUNDAY	MONDAY	TUESDAY	WEDNESDAY	THURSDAY	FRIDAY	SATURDAY
			1 9 tishri	**2** 10 tishri	**3** 11 tishri	**4** 12 tishri
			KOL NIDRE	YIZKOR YOM KIPPUR		Ha'azinu
5 13 tishri	**6** 14 tishri	**7** 15 tishri	**8** 16 tishri	**9** 17 tishri	**10** 18 tishri	**11** 19 tishri
	EREV SUKKOT	SUKKOT	SUKKOT	INTERMEDIATE DAY	INTERMEDIATE DAY	INTERMEDIATE DAY
12 20 tishri	**13** 21 tishri CANADIAN THANKSGIVING COLUMBUS DAY INDIGENOUS PEOPLES DAY	**14** 22 tishri	**15** 23 tishri	**16** 24 tishri	**17** 25 tishri	**18** 26 tishri
INTERMEDIATE DAY	INTERMEDIATE DAY	SHEMINI ATZERET	SIMCHAT TORAH			Breshit
19 27 tishri	**20** 28 tishri	**21** 29 tishri	**22** 30 tishri	**23** 1 cheshvan	**24** 2 cheshvan	**25** 3 cheshvan
			ROSH CHODESH	ROSH CHODESH		Noach
26 4 cheshvan	**27** 5 cheshvan	**28** 6 cheshvan	**29** 7 cheshvan	**30** 8 cheshvan	**31** 9 cheshvan	

November

5786
2025

cheshvan
kislev

SUNDAY	MONDAY	TUESDAY	WEDNESDAY	THURSDAY	FRIDAY	SATURDAY
						1 10 cheshvan
						Lech Lecha
2 11 cheshvan	**3** 12 cheshvan	**4** 13 cheshvan	**5** 14 cheshvan	**6** 15 cheshvan	**7** 16 cheshvan	**8** 17 cheshvan
						Vayera
9 18 cheshvan	**10** 19 cheshvan	**11** 20 cheshvan CANADIAN REMEMBERANCE DAY VETERANS DAY	**12** 21 cheshvan	**13** 22 cheshvan	**14** 23 cheshvan	**15** 24 cheshvan
						Chaye Sarah
16 25 cheshvan	**17** 26 cheshvan	**18** 27 cheshvan	**19** 28 cheshvan	**20** 29 cheshvan	**21** 1 kislev	**22** 2 kislev
				SIGD	ROSH CHODESH	Toldot
23 3 kislev	**24** 4 kislev	**25** 5 kislev	**26** 6 kislev	**27** 7 kislev	**28** 8 kislev	**29** 9 kislev
30 10 kislev				THANKSGIVING		Vayetzei

December

5786 / 2025
kislev / tevet

SUNDAY	MONDAY	TUESDAY	WEDNESDAY	THURSDAY	FRIDAY	SATURDAY
	1 11 kislev	**2** 12 kislev	**3** 13 kislev	**4** 14 kislev	**5** 15 kislev	**6** 16 kislev *Vayishlach*
7 17 kislev	**8** 18 kislev	**9** 19 kislev	**10** 20 kislev	**11** 21 kislev	**12** 22 kislev	**13** 23 kislev *Vayeshev*
14 24 kislev EREV HANUKKAH	**15** 25 kislev HANUKKAH	**16** 26 kislev *Vayeshev* HANUKKAH	**17** 27 kislev HANUKKAH	**18** 28 kislev HANUKKAH	**19** 29 kislev HANUKKAH	**20** 30 kislev *Miketz* ROSH CHODESH HANUKKAH
21 1 tevet ROSH CHODESH HANUKKAH	**22** 2 tevet HANUKKAH	**23** 3 tevet	**24** 4 tevet	**25** 5 tevet CHRISTMAS DAY	**26** 6 tevet	**27** 7 tevet *Vayigash*
28 8 tevet	**29** 9 tevet	**30** 10 tevet FAST OF 10TH OF TEVET	**31** 11 tevet			

KAR-BEN CALENDARS

At Judaica and bookstores or call **800-4-KARBEN (800-452-7236) or www.karben.com**

MY VERY OWN JEWISH CALENDAR

Attractive, amusing, and informative 16-month wall calendar with ample space for daily reminders. Each year features all-new facts, photos, recipes, and trivia. Now in full color. (Sept.–Dec.) Opens to 12" x 18".

JUMBO JEWISH CALENDAR

Use it as a desk blotter . . . hang it on your wall. Each date box has seven square inches of writing space for scheduling and reminders. Perfect for the busy home, classroom, or Jewish center. "Year-at-a-glance" on every page. 13 months (Sept.–Sept.) 17" x 22".

MINI JEWISH CALENDAR

Checkbook-size Jewish calendar for your purse or pocket. Always know when the holidays are coming. Space to jot down appointments and reminders. 13 months (Sept.–Sept.) Folds to 3" x 6".

EXECUTIVE JEWISH CALENDAR

A popular notebook-style calendar, perfect for home or office, desk or briefcase. Each month is a double-page spread with lots of room for appointments. Laminated cover. "Year-at-a-glance" on every page. 17 months (Aug.–Dec.) Opens to 17" x 11".

DIGITAL JEWISH CALENDAR

Kar-Ben's popular calendar now available in digital format. Customize it with your school or organization's special dates and reminders, and then print or e-mail to colleagues. Designed for use on both PC and Mac. 16 months (Sept.–Dec.). Order online only at www.karben.com.

All calendars are monthly planners with U.S., Canadian, and Jewish holidays, Shabbat Torah portions, and a candlelighting chart for major U.S. and Canadian cities.

© 2024 by Kar-Ben Publishing, a division of Lerner Publishing Group

CANDLELIGHTING CHART

		ATLANTA	BALTIMORE	BOSTON	CHICAGO	CLEVELAND	DALLAS	DENVER	LAKEWOOD	LOS ANGELES	MIAMI	MINNEAPOLIS	NEW YORK	PHILADELPHIA	PHOENIX	ST. LOUIS	WASHINGTON	MONTREAL	TORONTO
September	6	7:37	7:10	6:50	6:56	7:32	7:26	7:04	7:01	6:53	7:16	7:21	7:01	7:05	6:28	7:04	7:11	7:03	7:25
	13	7:28	6:59	6:38	6:44	7:20	7:17	6:52	6:50	6:43	7:08	7:08	6:49	6:53	6:18	6:53	7:00	6:50	7:12
	20	7:18	6:47	6:26	6:32	7:08	7:07	6:41	6:38	6:33	7:00	6:55	6:37	6:42	6:08	6:42	6:49	6:36	6:59
	27	7:08	6:36	6:13	6:20	6:56	6:58	6:29	6:26	6:23	6:53	6:41	6:25	6:30	5:59	6:30	6:38	6:23	6:46
October	4	6:59	6:25	6:01	6:08	6:44	6:49	6:18	6:15	6:14	6:45	6:28	6:14	6:19	5:49	6:20	6:27	6:09	6:34
	11	6:49	6:14	5:49	5:56	6:33	6:40	6:07	6:04	6:05	6:38	6:16	6:03	6:08	5:40	6:09	6:16	5:56	6:21
	18	6:41	6:04	5:38	5:45	6:22	6:31	5:57	5:53	5:56	6:31	6:03	5:52	5:57	5:32	5:59	6:06	5:44	6:10
	25	6:33	5:55	5:28	5:35	6:12	6:24	5:47	5:44	5:48	6:25	5:52	5:42	5:48	5:24	5:50	5:57	5:33	5:59
November	1	6:26	5:46	5:18	5:26	6:02	6:17	5:39	5:35	5:41	6:20	5:42	5:33	5:39	5:17	5:41	5:48	5:22	5:49
	8	5:20	4:39	4:10	4:17	4:54	5:11	4:31	4:28	4:35	5:16	4:33	4:25	4:32	5:11	4:34	4:41	4:13	4:40
	15	5:16	4:33	4:03	4:11	4:48	5:07	4:25	4:21	4:30	5:13	4:25	4:19	4:25	5:07	4:29	4:35	4:05	4:33
	22	5:12	4:28	3:58	4:06	4:43	5:04	4:21	4:17	4:27	5:11	4:19	4:14	4:21	5:04	4:24	4:31	3:59	4:28
	29	5:11	4:26	3:55	4:02	4:40	5:02	4:18	4:14	4:25	5:11	4:15	4:11	4:18	5:02	4:22	4:28	3:55	4:24
December	6	5:10	4:25	3:53	4:01	4:38	5:02	4:17	4:13	4:25	5:11	4:13	4:10	4:17	5:02	4:21	4:27	3:53	4:22
	13	5:12	4:25	3:54	4:02	4:39	5:04	4:18	4:13	4:26	5:13	4:13	4:11	4:18	5:03	4:22	4:28	3:53	4:22
	20	5:14	4:28	3:56	4:04	4:41	5:06	4:20	4:16	4:29	5:16	4:16	4:13	4:20	5:06	4:24	4:31	3:55	4:25
	27	5:18	4:32	4:00	4:08	4:46	5:10	4:24	4:20	4:33	5:20	4:20	4:17	4:24	5:10	4:28	4:35	3:59	4:29
January	3	5:23	4:38	4:06	4:14	4:51	5:15	4:30	4:26	4:38	5:25	4:26	4:23	4:30	5:15	4:34	4:40	4:05	4:35
	10	5:29	4:44	4:13	4:21	4:58	5:21	4:37	4:32	4:44	5:30	4:34	4:30	4:37	5:21	4:40	4:47	4:13	4:42
	17	5:36	4:52	4:21	4:29	5:06	5:28	4:44	4:40	4:51	5:35	4:42	4:37	4:44	5:27	4:48	4:54	4:22	4:51
	24	5:43	5:00	4:30	4:38	5:15	5:34	4:52	4:48	4:57	5:40	4:52	4:46	4:52	5:34	4:55	5:02	4:31	5:00
	31	5:49	5:08	4:39	4:47	5:23	5:41	5:00	4:57	5:04	5:46	5:02	4:54	5:01	5:41	5:04	5:10	4:42	5:09
February	7	5:56	5:16	4:48	4:56	5:32	5:47	5:09	5:05	5:11	5:51	5:12	5:03	5:09	5:47	5:12	5:18	4:52	5:19
	14	6:03	5:24	4:57	5:04	5:41	5:54	5:17	5:13	5:18	5:55	5:22	5:12	5:17	5:54	5:19	5:26	5:02	5:28
	21	6:09	5:32	5:06	5:13	5:50	6:00	5:25	5:21	5:24	6:00	5:32	5:20	5:25	6:00	5:27	5:34	5:12	5:38
	28	6:15	5:40	5:15	5:22	5:58	6:05	5:33	5:29	5:30	6:04	5:41	5:28	5:33	6:06	5:35	5:42	5:22	5:47
March	7	6:21	5:47	5:23	5:30	6:06	6:11	5:40	5:37	5:36	6:07	5:51	5:36	5:41	6:12	5:42	5:49	5:31	5:56
	14	7:26	6:54	6:31	6:38	7:14	7:16	6:48	6:44	6:42	7:11	7:00	6:44	6:48	6:17	6:49	6:56	6:41	7:05
	21	7:32	7:01	6:39	6:46	7:22	7:21	6:55	6:52	6:47	7:14	7:09	6:51	6:56	6:22	6:56	7:03	6:50	7:13
	28	7:37	7:08	6:47	6:54	7:30	7:26	7:02	6:59	6:53	7:17	7:18	6:58	7:03	6:28	7:02	7:10	6:59	7:22
April	4	7:42	7:15	6:55	7:01	7:37	7:31	7:09	7:06	6:58	7:21	7:27	7:06	7:10	6:33	7:09	7:16	7:08	7:30
	11	7:47	7:22	7:03	7:09	7:45	7:36	7:16	7:13	7:03	7:24	7:35	7:13	7:17	6:38	7:16	7:23	7:17	7:38
	18	7:53	7:29	7:11	7:17	7:52	7:41	7:23	7:20	7:09	7:27	7:44	7:20	7:24	6:43	7:22	7:30	7:26	7:47
	25	7:58	7:36	7:19	7:24	8:00	7:46	7:30	7:28	7:14	7:31	7:53	7:28	7:31	6:48	7:29	7:37	7:35	7:55
May	2	8:03	7:43	7:27	7:32	8:08	7:52	7:37	7:35	7:20	7:34	8:02	7:35	7:38	6:54	7:36	7:44	7:44	8:03
	9	8:09	7:49	7:35	7:40	8:15	7:57	7:44	7:42	7:25	7:38	8:10	7:42	7:45	6:59	7:42	7:50	7:53	8:11
	16	8:14	7:56	7:42	7:47	8:22	8:02	7:51	7:48	7:30	7:42	8:19	7:49	7:52	7:04	7:49	7:57	8:01	8:19
	23	8:19	8:02	7:49	7:54	8:29	8:07	7:57	7:55	7:35	7:45	8:26	7:56	7:58	7:09	7:55	8:03	8:09	8:26
	30	8:24	8:07	7:55	8:00	8:35	8:11	8:02	8:00	7:40	7:49	8:33	8:01	8:04	7:14	8:00	8:08	8:16	8:33
June	6	8:28	8:12	8:00	8:05	8:40	8:15	8:07	8:05	7:44	7:52	8:38	8:06	8:08	7:18	8:04	8:13	8:22	8:38
	13	8:31	8:16	8:04	8:08	8:43	8:18	8:11	8:09	7:47	7:55	8:42	8:10	8:12	7:21	8:08	8:16	8:26	8:42
	20	8:33	8:18	8:06	8:11	8:46	8:20	8:13	8:11	7:49	7:57	8:45	8:12	8:14	7:23	8:10	8:18	8:28	8:44
	27	8:34	8:19	8:07	8:11	8:46	8:21	8:14	8:12	7:50	7:58	8:45	8:13	8:15	7:24	8:11	8:19	8:29	8:45
July	4	8:33	8:18	8:06	8:10	8:45	8:21	8:13	8:11	7:50	7:58	8:44	8:12	8:14	7:23	8:10	8:18	8:27	8:44
	11	8:32	8:16	8:03	8:08	8:43	8:19	8:10	8:08	7:48	7:57	8:41	8:09	8:12	7:22	8:08	8:16	8:24	8:41
	18	8:29	8:12	7:58	8:03	8:38	8:16	8:06	8:04	7:45	7:55	8:36	8:05	8:08	7:19	8:04	8:12	8:19	8:36
	25	8:24	8:06	7:52	7:57	8:32	8:12	8:01	7:59	7:40	7:52	8:29	8:00	8:02	7:15	7:59	8:07	8:12	8:30
August	1	8:19	8:00	7:45	7:50	8:25	8:07	7:54	7:52	7:35	7:48	8:21	7:53	7:55	7:09	7:52	8:00	8:03	8:22
	8	8:13	7:52	7:36	7:41	8:17	8:01	7:46	7:44	7:28	7:43	8:11	7:44	7:47	7:03	7:45	7:53	7:54	8:13
	15	8:05	7:43	7:26	7:32	8:07	7:53	7:37	7:35	7:21	7:38	8:00	7:35	7:38	6:55	7:36	7:44	7:43	8:02
	22	7:57	7:33	7:16	7:21	7:57	7:45	7:27	7:25	7:13	7:31	7:49	7:25	7:28	6:47	7:27	7:34	7:31	7:51
	29	7:48	7:23	7:04	7:10	7:46	7:37	7:17	7:14	7:04	7:24	7:36	7:14	7:18	6:38	7:16	7:24	7:19	7:39
September	5	7:39	7:12	6:52	6:58	7:34	7:28	7:06	7:03	6:54	7:17	7:24	7:03	7:07	6:29	7:06	7:13	7:05	7:27
	12	7:29	7:01	6:40	6:46	7:22	7:18	6:54	6:52	6:45	7:09	7:10	6:51	6:55	6:20	6:55	7:02	6:52	7:14
	19	7:19	6:49	6:28	6:34	7:10	7:09	6:43	6:40	6:35	7:02	6:57	6:39	6:44	6:10	6:44	6:51	6:39	7:01
	26	7:10	6:38	6:15	6:22	6:58	7:00	6:31	6:28	6:25	6:54	6:44	6:27	6:32	6:00	6:32	6:40	6:25	6:49

This candlelighting chart is taken from *Hebcal Interactive Jewish Calendar* and is used by permission. The data is calculated based on Hebcal Version 3.4 by Danny Sadinoff and Web interface by Michael J. Radwin. If your city is not on the chart, you may look it up on the Hebcal website www.hebcal.com.

The Confidence Project

For over a decade, Carol Anne Baxter has helped thousands of women transform their lives with a unique blend of yoga, free form body movement, meditation and visualization techniques, and tapping (EFT - Emotional Freedom Technique). Carol uses her own personal experience combined with her years of training in yoga and healing modalities to help women realize what she discovered so many yoga classes ago: When we begin to invest in ourselves, we discover that anything is possible.

In addition to this journal, you can find *The Confidence Project Online Program*. This online course is designed to empower you to live your best life. The online program is full of guided yoga flows and meditations to help you take your journey to confidence to the next level. In addition, by joining the course you'll receive a playlist full of relaxing and meditative music perfect for playing in the background as you work your way through the reflective prompts in this journal.

Whether you choose to follow the entire course as Carol guides you back to your highest self, or simply visit a class or a meditation that speaks to you when you feel in need of a boost, this course will be there for you throughout your journey to confidence.

Learn more at www.CarolBaxter.ca/TheConfidenceProject and use the code TCPJOURNAL10 when signing up to save 10% off the full price of the course.

THE
CONFIDENCE
PROJECT

An empowering journey into a new you

Carol Anne Baxter

ISBN 978-1-54398-410-1

Editing by Sarah Dittmore, The Enlivened Collective
Cover & Book Design by Tanya Gupta, The Enlivened Collective
Photographs by Theresa Carter, Weddings and Media

Printed and bound by BookBaby
First printing September 2019

www.CarolBaxter.ca/TheConfidenceProject

Acknowledgements

This book was made possible by a team of people for whom I am in loving gratitude.

Sarah Dittmore and Tanya Gupta of The Enlivened Collection, thank you for helping me craft my vision into the beautiful story that it now is. You girls filled my heart with encouragement and loving guidance along this journey and I am so grateful.

Thank you to Theresa Carter, from Weddings and Media. The pictures throughout this book are all the creative vision of this wonderful woman. Theresa, from the bottom of my heart I thank you for all of the kindness, humour, and light that you shone on this project.

Thank you to my husband Craig, for always having the confidence in me to go further than I ever dreamed possible. You have literally helped to build my dreams into reality. I love you!

Thank you to my mom, for loving me unconditionally and teaching me that anything is possible.

The Flower of Life & Tabono: Visualizing The Confidence Project

"The Flower of Life" symbolizes creation and reminds us of the unity of everything. "*Tabono*" means "oar" or "paddle" in the Adinkra language of Western Africa and is a symbol of unity of purpose, strength, confidence and hard work to reach a destination or goal.

By bringing these sacrad images together, we hope The Confidence Project's symbol and what it stands for will inspire you throughout your journey of building your own self-confidence and living in universal harmony.

*This book is dedicated to my husband and my daughter
for their encouragement and love along the way.*

And to the the never ending journey of my infinite soul...

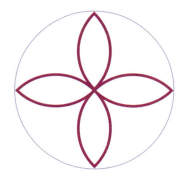

CONTENTS

Close your eyes and imagine the best version of you possible.
That's who you really are. Let go of any part of you that doesn't believe it.

- C. Assaad

BUILDING A NEW YOU

Close your eyes for a moment.
Think back to when you were a child. Who was your favourite superhero? Who did you look up too?

Now take a deep breath and tap into how you felt when you used to see this superhero. What did they represent to you? Perhaps feelings of excitement, awe, wonder, and power ran through you. Believe it or not, you are more like that superhero than you realize. We all inhabit the qualities we admire in other people; we just haven't claimed them yet.

My favourite superhero was Wonder Woman. She represented strength, compassion, beauty, and out-of-this-world abilities that left me in awe every time I watched her show. Most of all, I admired Wonder Woman because she was strong and confident in who she was; I wanted to grow up to be just like her.

We are constantly sending out messages about who we think we are. If we believe we lack confidence, are not good enough, or are not worthy of abundance, our world will respond with these exact circumstances. We are the creators of everything in our reality. We just haven't been conditioned to believe this. Most of our limited thinking and belief patterns are unconscious and have been with us for years. We don't even realize how often we think and act in certain ways; ways that create our entire reality.

In the stories the superhero always takes a journey. They slowly realize their potential for magic and begin to come into their powers, then progressively activate these powers as their inherent belief in themself deepens. Eventually something happens in this journey that halts the superhero or instills them with self-doubt. Moving through this internal conflict, the superhero arrives on the other side more powerful and confident than ever before. The journey has made them

question, doubt, and move through conflict. They are faced with fear, but in the end they become fully present, fully alive, and fully confident in the greatest version of themselves.

This, in essence, is the journey we all take in life as we come to recognize our inherent greatness and power to be whomever we wish.

In order to transform our world and claim our most confident selves, we must undertake a journey of reconnection to our bodies, understand how to release the past, tap into our emotions in a safe and fluid way, and bond with our spirit selves. The symbiotic relationship of these three components raises our consciousness and generates an awareness of who we truly are. It forms the most important relationship we will ever embrace; our relationship with ourselves. Once we form this relationship, we become more consciously aware of how to change our own vibration and create the life of our dreams.

A little bit about me...

I was born the year of the tiger. My mom wrote in my baby book that, as an infant, I used to growl like a tiger and they never understood why. Now, looking back, I smile when I read that. I believe this was a reflection of who I was to be in the world: a driven, courageous woman who shines from the inside out when empowering others.

I am a libra; a believer of all things energy, divine guidance, and the innate power of being anything that you deem impossible but truly wish you could be.

My life has been my complete creation (as has yours). Every hard lesson had a silver lining and anything I truly desired, I manifested to come true. This pure fact alone affirms my belief in the inherent power we each have to be whomever we dream of being.

I define who I am in the world as a yoga teacher, an energy worker, and a life coach. I am also a shamanic practitioner, a yoga teacher training facilitator, a reiki master, an emotional freedom technique practitioner, a wife, and a proud mom.

I have spent years researching and learning how to connect to my body and my soul. I have been on a path of discovering how to release self-judgment, past experiences, and limiting beliefs in order to step into the truth of who I really am. I have craved the essence of accepting all that I am while moving away from self-judgment and fear.

The road I have travelled thus far has been anything but easy. It has included many emotional twists and turns in order to move through long held fears and step into my truth. It is amazing for me to think back and remember when the mere thought of standing up in front of a room to deliver a speech left me riddled with anxiety for days prior. My deep fears about judgment from other people kept me small for a long time.

Fast forward ten years and I am now the host of my own television show, the owner of three yoga studios, a yoga teacher trainer facilitator, and a public speaker who discusses the power of energy and healing at large corporate events. This eventful road I have travelled has taught me how to open my heart, feel my emotions, release self-judgment, and live from a place of empowerment I never dreamed possible.

For more than a decade I have worked with a wide variety of students, be it in my yoga classes, through my teacher trainings, or with personal clients. Almost all of these students struggle with a lack of belief in themselves. It seems we have all been conditioned to ignore our inner calling and deny ourselves the confidence we need to travel the path of self-discovery.

Many of us exist in jobs we don't like, relationships that don't serve us, and the general feeling that we can't do much about our current situation. We often learn to 'just live with it' and accept our own inherent dissatisfaction. This feeling of defeat and simply moving through life without passion or fulfilment stems from a lack of core belief in ourselves and not understanding that we can create whatever we wish to be and see in our worlds. Instead, we learn to follow the status quo and live with how things are, even when this causes us deep inner conflict.

Truth: many women suffer from a lack of belief in themselves and deny their ability to step into the greatness of who they truly are. Many of us live with a fear inside that keeps us from stepping forward or making a change in our lives. This fear comes from judgement of oneself, the fear of judgement from other people, fear of making mistakes, and limiting beliefs that we formed as children. Quite simply, women often grow up lacking the belief that they already are everything that they desire to be.

Many of us confront choices that test our confidence every single day. We either make a decision that is empowering or one that holds us back in fear. When we lack self confidence, we lack belief in who we are. Our true, beautiful essence becomes blocked as we grow used to giving away our power on a daily basis. Often, these habits begin in childhood and carry through into adulthood; that is a lot of years spent living in lack and fear.

Now let's turn to the other side of this spectrum and reconnect to that amazing feeling of empowerment and the picture in your mind of your most favourite superhero. Where do these light feelings of admiration come from?

Quite simply, they come from a deep inner connection to who we already are at our core. Our divine essence is powerful, strong, and confident; and she is waiting patiently to be seen and released.

How would it feel to stand firm in a decision? To speak your truth? To walk into a room and not worry about what other people think of you? To release self-judgment? To live with passion and connection to the things that matter most to you?

This journal has crossed your path for a reason. Its magical pages are lined with the cornerstones of growth and discovery that lead to living your most empowered life. It will take you back to the beginning and help to deconstruct the obstacles that are standing in the way of living your most fulfilled life. It will rebuild your chakra system and give you tools to use every single day to connect you deeper to the truth of who you are. A tool in your growth and a lighthouse on the path of discovery, *The Confidence Project* is designed to lead you back to your essence.

We are connected now. Our paths have energetically crossed and it thrills me that you are exploring this journal. I have become a part of your own self-discovery and that fills my heart with gratitude. I invite you to step into the greatness of who you are and explore this program with me.

Blessings...

Light...

Love...

And connection on the path home to you.

Yours Truly,

Carol Anne Baxter

What is Self-Confidence?

I took a random poll from my students, clients, teachers, family, and friends. These are some of the words and phrases that they associated with self-confidence:

- Belief in myself and in my capabilities.

- The undoubted assurance that I am moving in the right direction.

- It means feeling free, comfortable, and happy in my own skin. Loving every part of myself, the light and the dark, and not being afraid to shine.

- Self-confidence means feelings of joy, empowerment, and acceptance of myself.

- Self-confidence is when you feel good about yourself and the decisions you make without second guessing and without worry of what others will think. It is having the strength and faith in yourself to move forward with what you believe regardless of the obstacles in your way.

- Trust in myself, my abilities, and not requiring validation from someone else.

- Self-confidence means self-assurance, no self-doubt or judgement. Not being afraid to be who I am. Confident in my own skin. Trusting myself when nobody else does. Self-confidence is powerful.

- The measure in the quality of the relationship you have with yourself. It is the byproduct of your personal review in the quality of the thoughts you are producing, noticing, and accepting about how you arrive in each moment of your day.

- Self-confidence to me means being happy with who I am and not needing validation from anyone or anything.

- To have trust in yourself in a positive manner!

- Self-confidence means you are comfortable with yourself, inside and out. You feel true love and respect for yourself as a human being and a soul. It's the ability to see the greatness in other people and other things while acknowledging your differences as well. It's seeing yourself as capable, unique, and perfect just as you are. Self-confidence is your true inner beauty shining through.

Defining Self-Confidence

Self-confidence is an unwavering belief in yourself and in your capabilities. It is the undoubted assurance that we believe deeply in ourselves and the direction we are moving, no matter what other people think. And here is the other secret: once we become grounded in who we are, we naturally begin to care less about what others think, and we learn how to release self judgment, moving forward towards our goals and who we are meant to be at lighting speed. We begin to create the life we are meant to live.

Who was your favourite superhero as a child? List all of the qualities they have. In what ways do you embody these qualities?

_____

_____

_____

_____

_____

_____

What does self-confidence mean to you?

_____

_____

_____

_____

_____

How would you like self-confidence to change your life?

_____

_____

_____

_____

_____

_____

_____

_____

What is your intention or goal in moving through this sacred journal?

_____

_____

_____

_____

_____

_____

_____

_____

_____

_____

_____

Confidence Action Steps

Simple Ways to Begin Your Journey Toward Self - Confidence

Creating Your Avatar. One of the most powerful tools you will ever learn and condition yourself to practice is the art of visualization. Visualization has the power to create anything you truly desire and see yourself to be and experience. Anything that has ever become a reality for you, either positive or negative, always began with an image in the mind.

Learning to create your own personal avatar of the highest vision you have of yourself is the first Confidence Action Tip of this journal.

Building avatars has always been my own secret power. I use them personally and I create them when I am helping my friends manifest something new in their lives. Every single avatar I have ever created has become true; that's why I am so happy to help you begin to create your own.

The more you see yourself as what you'd like to become, and act as if what you want is already there, the more you'll activate those dormant forces that will collaborate to transform your dream into your reality ... - Wayne Dyer

My Idealized Self Meditation. Create sacred space around you. Light a candle, close the door, burn some incense. Have your journal close by.

- Close your eyes and move into your favourite breath practice. Notice your inhale and exhale and your body responding to the awareness of your breath.
- Place your left hand on your heart and notice its rhythm. Can you count the beats to your heart? Imagine every inhale is moving directly into the centre of your heart and every exhale is releasing old energy and resistance.
- Call to mind your favourite place in nature. Feel the earth beneath you and the sun above you. Connect to both beautiful energies.
- Begin to envision your greatest self. What is she doing? What does she look like? How does she feel? See her in the activity that represents the you without limits.

- Begin to embody the same feeling that the image is showing you. Feel it in your body, connect to the energy it creates inside of you. Let a soft smile embrace you as you embody this image.
- This is YOU. This is confident, limitless, inspiring, beautiful, and fearless YOU. Connect to her in whatever way feels right for you. Hold her hands, look into her eyes, and breathe life into this image.
- Stay in this meditation and continue to see yourself in the most idealized state of begin and feeling. Breathe life into this image and exhale any doubts or fears.
- When you feel complete and connected to the truth of this new vibration that is you, take one deep breath in, one long exhale out, and open your eyes.

Journal about what the new you looks like. What is she wearing? What is she doing? What are the feelings she is embodying? Is she standing near a beach? A forest? On top of a mountain?

And most importantly, how is she feeling? Does she stand in confidence, joy, and peace? Get very specific about your greatest self. She is the new you.

_____

_____

_____

_____

_____

_____

_____

_____

_____

_____

_____

_____

_____

_____

_____

_____

_____

_____

_____

This beautiful image will shift and shape itself throughout the process of this journal as you become naturally clearer about how you see yourself living your most fulfilled life.

Use this space to draw, sketch, or design your avatar. Be as detailed as possible. Explore what she looks like, where she is, and what she's doing in the image.

A Daily Meditation Into Your Truth. I began exploring kundalini yoga many years ago. I find it to be a mind-body-spirit-connecting and soul-shifting practice.

One of the things explored in kundalini yoga are mantras. Mantras are sounds that connect us with different levels of consciousness. *Sat Nam* is one of the most basic mantras used in Kundalini yoga. *Sat* means the "truth" and *Nam* means "identity". Together, *Sat Nam* essentially means "my name is truth". This phrase is repeated in meditations and affirmation practices to remind you of your soul essence. Saying this phrase even once changes something inside of you and accesses a resonant power attached to the vibration of the mantra.

One of the essential steps in *The Confidence Project* is connecting to who you truly are underneath all of the things you think you are. Most of us are all familiar with the phrase, "The truth will set you free." The question is, how do we begin the steps to get there? Learning and adopting a *Sat Nam* mantra is a great first action step.

This mantra has the power to reprogram your subconscious mind so that old wounds and programs no longer get in the way of self-realization and self-confidence. It does so by changing the projection of our minds.

Enjoy the meditation below to help align and connect you to who you are. This is to be practiced daily, preferably first thing in the morning.

1. Sit tall, either on a pillow or bolster to support your hips, or sitting back on your heels.

2. Straighten your arms and interlace your hands above you with the thumbs crossing (left over right for ladies; the opposite for men).

3. Close your eyes and take three deep breaths in through the nose and out through the mouth, giving all doubt, all hesitation, and all stress back to the universe.

4. Inhale as you say out loud (or in your mind), "*Sat*".

5. As you exhale say out loud (or in your mind), "*Nam*".

6. Repeat for 1- 3 minutes.

7. When finished, release your grip and breathe in and out, observing your physical body and the quality of your mind.

Part One

My Amazing Body

MY AMAZING BODY

The Sacred Vessel of my Journey

We walk around in a pretty fantastic space; our body. However, we can often lose our connection to our body or forget the magical place that it actually is. And it is truly magical. Our body holds all of our unprocessed thoughts, emotions, memories, and stories. It is also a beautiful container of creation, possibility, and wonder. In addition, it is our main vessel of transportation as we navigate through the journey that is our life.

When we begin to question our path, who we are, where we want to move, or the great vision we have for ourselves, we must explore the relationship we have with our physical form and become friends with her once again.

When we are born, we are born whole. We are complete souls with eyes wide open and eager to embark on a journey in this world. Nothing can stop us or stand in our way. As children, we are deeply connected to our body and our emotions. It is in this phase of life that we begin to admire superheroes, our elder siblings, close family friends, and our parents. We are able to move and express ourselves freely as things come in and out of our awareness. That is, so long as we are not told by our caregivers that expressing our emotions is unacceptable.

Consider this: the soul that we are born with as a baby is the same soul that we are at age 85. Our soul is, in essence, timeless. We are born deeply connected, empowered, and confident. So what happens to those amazing feelings? Where do they go? They are still inside of us, but the outside world, along with our subconscious beliefs and patterns, holds us back.

This section of the journal is meant to reconnect you to the sacred temple of your body. Together, we will explore the chakra system and take a journey back in time to understand the development of each of our chakras. The meditations, energy routines, practices, and tips included with each chakra are designed to stimulate and heal your energetic system, clearing out old patterns and ways of being so that you may become grounded in who you truly are.

There is a lot of information to digest and explore within each chakra; take your time. Perhaps you embrace and allow the practices for each one to be with you for a week or two before you move on. Remember, this is your time to work on you. There is no rushing greatness.

The Root Chakra

Our root chakra begins its development between the ages of 0-7. It is during this crucial period that we begin to form agreements about the world and our place in it. These agreements are created around the opinions and beliefs that our parents, siblings, and close friends share.

Our root chakra begins its development between the ages of 0-7. It is during this crucial period that we begin to form agreements about the world and our place in it. These agreements are created around the opinions and beliefs that our parents, siblings, and close friends share.

The Root Chakra is the foundation that holds a home. Before I truly understood what chakras meant, I didn't value the importance of connecting to the earth. I felt this way for many years and part of me resisted the practice of grounding. Thankfully, the more I engaged in my practice of yoga, and as my knowledge of the spiritual world deepened, I began to understand how important it is to feel grounded. When we are grounded in the earth, we are connected more deeply to who we are. We naturally enhance our physical, mental, and emotional well-being and create a sound way of thinking.

In today's world, we live amongst constant technology that distracts and over-stimulates us, concrete buildings that make it hard to see the sun, and an overwhelming amount of cell phone and computer activity. Some of us get up in the morning, get into our car through the garage, drive to work, park underground, and sit in an office all day long. We don't even get a chance to experience fresh air or the ground beneath our feet. Add in the constant interactions with our cell phones, microwaves, and other forms of technology that give us electromagnetic radiation (which can negatively affect our cells and our DNA) and it is no wonder we are often left feeling unbalanced.

Let's face it; the world is not set up to naturally connect us to the earth. When we feel unbalanced in life or unclear and unsure about decisions or situations, the best thing we can do is find our own way of connecting to the earth and balancing our Root Chakra.

When this chakra is balanced we are able to harness our courage and move forward into our life goals and aspirations with a strong foundation. We don't give in to insecurities or fears surrounding finances, health, or where we are headed in our lives. Instead, we feel supported and confident in who we truly are. We are aware of our real needs and desires and the path that we must take in order to fulfill them.

A Note on Chakras

Chakras are spinning disks of energy that interact with different physiological and neurological systems in the body. I like to describe them as energy centres within us that help regulate our emotions, our immune system, and even our organ function.

We have seven main chakras throughout our body; beginning from the pelvic floor and traveling up the spine to the crown of the head.

Each chakra takes seven years to develop. The first chakra is the root chakra and its position in the body is at the pelvic floor. This chakra begins its development when we are still in the womb.

When our chakras are out of balance, we are out of balance. The strengthening of each energy centre in the body is crucial for bringing balance to the body, mind, and spirit as well as moving you forward on your path to being the strong, confident person that you already are.

The Root Chakra is the first chakra and the foundational base that all of our other chakras build upon. The high, positive charge of the energy of the Root Chakra is necessary for us to grow into any vision we have for ourselves.

The root chakra lies at the base of the spine and the pelvic floor and is symbolic of the colour red. If you were to imagine you were building a house, the Root Chakra would be the foundation. The development of this chakra begins between the ages of 0-7 when we naturally attach to our parents and siblings. This chakra is fulfilled when our basic needs are being met such as food, water, shelter, and safety. As an infant and then a child, if your caregivers gave you what you needed to survive with consistency, then you generally should feel safe and secure in the world. If you did not receive these basic needs, you may suffer from feelings of ungroundedness, unworthiness, and fear about stepping out of your comfort zone. This is a big step backward in the development of self-confidence. As we grow into our adulthood, this chakra can be underdeveloped if we are unhappy in our careers or feel we lack in any relationship with our immediate family members or close tribe of friends.

Muladhara
The Root Chakra

Meaning:
    -mula = root/base/foundation
    -adhara = support/basis/receptacle
Colour: Red
Location: Base of the Spine, Lowest Chakra
Element: Earth
Mantra: LAM

Can you remember how you felt between the age of 0 and 7? Most of us don't believe we can, but the truth is still in us. Journaling about these years can help you remember situations that occurred and how they caused you to see the world and your place in it in a certain light.

Who were your favourite people during these early years? What were your favourite foods? How were you exploring the world at this age?

_____

_____

_____

_____

_____

_____

_____

_____

_____

_____

_____

_____

_____

Do you have any memories from this time that are sad or disempowering? Describe as much as you can remember about these moments and how they made you feel.

_____

_____

_____

_____

_____

_____

_____

What methods do you use today to ground yourself? What methods could you use?

_____

_____

_____

_____

_____

_____

_____

_____

_____

Close your eyes and breathe into the creation of your personal avatar. Which aspects of the root chakra are important for her to feel on a daily basis?

_____

_____

_____

_____

_____

_____

_____

_____

_____

_____

_____

_____

_____

_____

_____

_____

*Create the highest, grandest vision possible for your life, because
you always become what you believe ...* - Unknown

Confidence Action Steps

Simple Ways to Open, Heal, and Clear your Root Chakra

Walk in the woods. Nature holds so much energetic power. Think about the things that were disempowering between the ages of 0-7 and breathe them out of your body as you walk amongst the trees and all of nature. What are you ready to let go of?

Stand on the earth barefoot and breathe deeply. Imagine your feet have roots and those roots are growing downward and grounding deep into the centre of the earth. Send love to Mother Earth and wait to feel her return that love to you. Trust me, you will feel it.

Repeat these affirmations everyday:

> "I am safe"
> "The universe provides for me"
> "I am empowered in my own truth"

Affirmations are important because they affirm a new belief system. Take time each day to pick one that resonates with you and let that be the theme of your day. When I first began affirming new beliefs, I would place them on a sticky note and take it with me wherever I went. It would be the first thing I would think about when I woke up in the morning and I continued to say it out loud, or mindfully remember it, throughout the day. For the ones that were hardest for me to say, I would stare at myself in the mirror and repeat them over and over again until I felt that they were true. The key is repetition. Repeat, repeat, repeat. It is so important to commit to a new way of being and feeling if we desire to become the creators of our lives.

Close your eyes and bring in the image of your avatar.

How grounded is she to the earth? Can you feel a connection that creates a stability and assurity in who she is?

My Crystal Earth Chords Meditation

Sit down with a straight spine and your feet connected to the ground beneath you. Take three full, deep, centred breaths; draw the inhale through the nose and release the exhale through the mouth.

With every exhale, give away all of your thoughts, stresses, worries, or anything that is occupying space inside of you. Imagine two long chords beginning at the centre of each foot and reaching down to the centre of the earth. Your chords can be any colour, shape, or size you imagine; I always imagine my chords as silver and twisted with beautiful quartz crystals throughout. Visualize energy flowing where the chords connect with the earth; this energy is clear, crisp, and renewing.

Begin to breathe out any toxic, old, or stale energy that resides in your physical form and feel it flow from your feet, down your chords, and into the earth's centre. You are giving the earth your old energy so that it can be recycled and made anew.

As you breathe in, imagine that new, crystal clean energy is making its way back up your chords, into your feet and spreading all through your body. Let this energy take on a colour and continue to breathe it in until it refreshes every cell of your body. Allow your grounding chords to take on different shapes and colours; do the same with the energy that you bring into your body.

Repeat this exercise of releasing old energy and taking in the new as many times as feels necessary. The more you practice this, the more you will feel this meditation's positive effects. You will experience feelings of positivity, support, and love as you ground into and deepen your connection with Mother Earth. I recommend practicing this exercise every single day to strengthen your root chakra and experience the secure sensation of grounding.

Energy Classes for Confidence

When I began taking regular yoga classes, I was completely hooked on the feelings I experienced. I loved how my body and mind felt whenever I practiced. But as this practice deepened and my teaching expanded, so did my awareness of energy and its power. I started to understand how working with the chakras and practicing kundalini yoga can be transformative.

There is SO much power in kundalini yoga and energy work. We live day to day with old, stagnant energy that can keep us at a low vibration. Kundalini yoga helps us pull the old stuff up and out, making room for new vitality and life force. When we are blocked or unbalanced, our actions and decision making come from the realm of subconscious thought. This keeps us stuck in old habits and limiting beliefs. However, when we practice kundalini yoga, we naturally lift and transform this old energy and inhabit a more conscious space. This allows us to pursue our goals and better connect with our true selves.

After exploring these practices for myself, I developed the class I call 'Energy.' This class involves the elements of breath, ancient kundalini yoga, flow, and energy clearing. It is designed to help clear your body, mind, and spirit of negative emotions and begin to empower, heal, and build your most confident self.

Throughout this section of the journal, you will receive three Energy Class routines. Practice them at least one-to-three times a week and watch as your old energy transforms into vital life force. It is so important to do one thing each day that connects your body, mind, and spirit. If you cannot do the full class, pick one of the exercises in the sequence and commit to it first thing in the morning. It will change your vibe, guaranteed!

All of the routines, meditations, and exercises in this book are designed to raise your vibration, bringing you out of old patterns of behavior and into new conscious actions that move you towards being your best self, free of doubt and negativity. I encourage you to breathe through the things from the past that you wish to release from your physical and energetic body throughout these sequences. Use each practice as a clearing vessel to let go and move you one step closer to becoming your greatest self.

Energy Class for the Root Chakra

This class is designed to open, heal, and strengthen your root chakra. Breathe into your transformation through this practice. Every inhale takes in the new and every exhale releases the old. Think of the soles of your feet and imagine they have tiny openings that gather earth energy and carry it throughout your whole body. Connect to Gaia in this practice. As you heal yourself, you are also helping mother earth heal.

*All energy classes can be found in the Energy Class Appendix at the end of this journal.

Pass it Forward

Tools to empower your child's chakra development and help build their self-confidence

Make a weekly habit of walking with your child in nature. Connect with them; talk about school, chat about their friends... most of all, simply spend quality time together enjoying nature. Use this time to understand what is real for them at this stage of their lives.

Encourage the practice of breathing by teaching them to breathe in new energy and breath out any negativity they may feel. I make a practice of checking in with my daughter at the end of every school day. I want her to express how she feels about what's been true for her and at the same time teach her that she has the power within her to let it all go and remain perfect just as she is.

Encourage affirmation statements with your child such as: "I am enough," "I am strong," and "I am confident".

Remind them each day of the inherent power that lies within them.

Walk barefoot on the earth together.

Practice yoga with your child.

The Sacral Chakra

The second chakra is the sacral chakra. It lies three inches below the navel, at the centre of your lower belly. Its development begins between the ages of 8 and 14; its colour is orange. The element associated with the sacral chakra is water.

This chakra is associated with our emotional body. When it is open, we are expressive in our feelings and allow them to flow freely. It is also the home of our creative instincts and the expression of our sensual and sexual desires.

When we open this chakra, we can feel the world around us and understand what it means to experience happiness and true joy. It is at this stage that children begin to place greater importance on friendships, experience a wide range of emotions, and start to discover their own individual expression. If you felt you were unable to be creative, experience your feelings, and express yourself as a child, you may now suffer from feelings of shame, guilt, or consistent self-doubt. You may also have a very limited image of yourself.

My own experience with my sacral chakra came as I learned to embrace my expressive self. In my younger years, I always felt worried about my self-expression. I remember feeling unsure about stepping outside of the safe box I had created around myself. Being an extremely sensitive child, I was acutely aware of people's opinions. I did not want to disappoint anyone and my parents did not exactly encourage self-expression; naturally, I conformed to the way I was told things should be done and presented myself the way I thought people wanted me to. It wasn't until I began the practice of yoga that I was able to tap into my own creativity and ability to self-express. And wow, once you begin to tap into your own creative life force, it feels absolutely amazing!!

Svadhisthana
The Sacral Chakra

Meaning:
-sva/swa = one's own
-adhisthana = abode/seat
Colour: Orange
Location: Lower Abdomen, Second Chakra
Element: Water
Mantra: VAM

Take a deep breath. Close your eyes. Imagine yourself between the ages of 8 and 14. This was the time of developing your creativity, expression, and wonder. Journal about what you can call to mind here.

How was your creativity expressed between the ages of 8-14?

_____
_____
_____
_____
_____

Were you involved in art classes at this age? Could you paint, draw, colour, and create things freely? In what ways were you encouraged or discouraged to explore different forms of creative expression?

_____
_____
_____
_____
_____
_____

How were your ideas and feelings expressed? How were they received by your family, teachers, and friends?

_____

_____

_____

_____

_____

How confident do you feel about your self-image now?

_____

_____

_____

_____

_____

Your avatar expresses creativity… she feeds from a deep source of inspiration. List some of the ways the idealized image of you creates and expands her self-expression in the world.

_____

_____

_____

_____

_____

Confidence Action Steps

Simple Ways to Open, Heal, and Clear your Sacral Chakra

Get outside and enjoy being near open water. Allow your feet to simply dangle in the water; this will increase the flow of energy in your body.

Join an art class! Do this on your own, with a friend or significant other, or with your child. Allow yourself to explore something new and creative.

Explore your sensuality. Understand your feminine side and look for ways to nurture it. What makes you feel sensual?

Take baths… lots of them. This is my personal favourite for the sacral chakra. Add epson salts and baking soda to your bath to help cleanse your energetic field.

Begin to accept your feelings and allow them to flow through you. Every feeling we have is real and valid. Learning how to accept our feelings is an integral part of accepting who we are.

Repeat one or all of these affirmations every day. Pick the one that truly resonates with you and focus on it:

"I enjoy life fully"
"I am unique and filled with beauty"
"The world needs more of me"
"I am ready for positive change and for deep personal growth"
"My body is vibrant and I am comfortable inside of it"

Close your eyes and bring in the image of your avatar. How open and expressive is she? Does she move through the ebb and flow of life with grace and ease? Is she creative in her wardrobe? Does she engage in creative activities that make her heart sing?

Try Something New

This week, explore your own creative self-expression and pick an activity that you have always been interested in trying. Consider painting, sculpting, pottery, photography, cooking, or dancing. These are all fantastic ways to unleash our own creative genius. I guarantee you will find something new that you love!

Pass it Forward

Tools to empower your child's chakra development and help build their self-confidence

Look for signs of creative expression in your children at this age. Welcome it all. Understand your child is searching for ways to express their most natural self and some of it may catch you off guard. Breathe deeply and allow it to flow through them (and you). Keep in mind that self-image is developing at this stage. Confidence, or lack thereof, is beginning to show itself.

Who is your child's favourite superhero? Journal with your child about the qualities this super hero has. Remind your child she holds each of these qualities too. My daughter's favourite superhero is Supergirl and I remind her daily that she too has the strength and compassion of Supergirl.

Enforce a positive self-image as much as possible. Remind your child how unique and beautiful they are every single day.

Allow the expression of every single emotion your child has. It is in this phase of life where a child learns it is safe to express emotions.

Encourage affirmation statements with your child and yourself.

The Solar Plexus Chakra

The Solar Plexus Chakra is the third chakra and it is also called the personal power chakra. It is located in the upper part of the abdomen where the diaphragm rests. Its development begins between the ages of 15-21 and it is represented by the colour yellow. The element associated with this chakra is fire. When I think of this chakra, the words that comes to mind are transformation, change, and power.

This chakra is all about confidence and the seed of your will. A properly energized solar plexus chakra provides us with the strength to move forward in life and actualize our visions and goals. When this chakra is in the prime of its development, it causes us to begin determining our own value. Often, if we have had difficult experiences as a young child and as a teenager, we decide that we aren't 'good enough'. This belief impacts us for the rest of our lives.

Manipura
The Solar Plexus Chakra

Meaning:
   -mani = gem/jewel
   -pura = city
Colour: Yellow
Location: Above the Naval, Third Chakra
Element: Fire
Mantra: RAM

A closed solar plexus chakra can result in feelings of low self worth, close mindedness, judgment, and criticism. Your confidence may be shaky. Energizing and healing this chakra is key in recognizing your hidden self-confidence.

I love my mom dearly, and we have an amazing relationship, but like many of us, confidence was something she struggled with also. She was a product of bullying in school and that all too familiar feeling of not being good enough stuck with her from childhood onward. We are always influenced by what we see around us; as we grow and develop, we look to our parents for examples of how to be in the world. If our parents suffer from feelings of low self-worth, then we most likely will

as well. Remember, our parents didn't have the tools to release, heal, and empower themselves on another level as they were growing up which inevitably made it difficult, if not near-impossible, for them to empower their own children.

As a school girl, I always felt that I didn't fit in. This feeling began when I was a young child and carried through as I entered high school. When we have one negative experience around being 'not good enough' or 'not fitting in' as a young child, it most likely stays with us for life. My solar plexus chakra was most definitely not in its full energetic capacity as I moved through this phase of growth.

"I'm not good enough" is the one main limiting belief I work with adults on. Journal about this age and let your feelings rise to the surface. This can be a big one, but this practice can release everything that arises from your physical and energetic body.

What were your hopes and dreams at this age?

_____

_____

_____

_____

_____

_____

Did you play sports? How did it feel to win or lose?

_____

_____

_____

_____

_____

_____

_____

What did you consider to be your successes at this age? Your failures?

_____

_____

_____

_____

_____

_____

_____

_____

_____

How confident were you as an adolescent?

_____

_____

_____

_____

_____

_____

_____

_____

_____

_____

Confidence Action Steps

Simple Ways to Open, Heal, and Clear your Solar Plexus Chakra

Be outside. Get close to the sun. The more vitamin D we receive, the less likely we are to experience depression and anxiety.

Learn how to release your anger safely. When we do this, we free up blocked energy inside of us. Try kickboxing, a punching bag, writing, or even crying.

Strengthen your core as much as possible. Take a regular pilates class; make it a daily habit if you can. The core is the seat of this chakra. The more we strengthen it, the more confident we become.

Repeat these affirmations every day, or the one that speaks to you the most:

> "I respect and honour who I am"
> "I am limitless"
> "I believe in myself"
> "My positive visions about myself become my reality"
> "I am powerful beyond measure"

Close your eyes and invoke the image of your avatar. Do you see her radiating with will, determination, and strength? Write down the qualities you see in her that stem from the empowerment of this chakra.

Feel the Fear... Then do it Anyway

This week, take a risk and do something you wouldn't normally do. Our routines are our safety zones and they don't encourage the lift off into the great unknown that gives us confidence. Try something new and journal about how it felt.

Choose to wear something that you really love but are afraid of being seen in. This can be a big one for a lot of us. I used to hide behind clothes I felt helped me fit into the crowd when my heart was actually singing to wear a beautiful dress or a brightly coloured shirt. When we make simple choices that feed our souls, and step out of the paradigm of fear, we feel absolutely AMAZING. We feel that we have conquered something that has held us captive for a long time; that feeling brings us confidence and freedom.

Begin to take note of your posture on a daily basis. Do you stand tall with your shoulders held back or do you naturally concave your shoulders forward and drop your head slightly? Posture is everything. When we stand tall, pulling our shoulders back and lifting the crown of the head to gaze forward at people, it sends our body and the world a message about who we are. It may seem simple, but this change can begin to naturally enhance your solar plexus chakra and strengthen your willpower. Beginning today, take notice of how you are presenting yourself to the world and begin to initiate this change.

Energy Class for the Sacral and Solar Plexus Chakras

This is an energy class that is meant to open, heal, and strengthen your sacral and solar plexus chakras. Each exercise will tap into the field of energy that rests in these areas of the body so that you can let go of the past and gently draw in the new. Allow memories, doubts, and disbeliefs to show themselves to you. Without sitting in judgment of yourself, forgive everything, come back to your breath, and begin again.

*All energy classes can be found in the Energy Class Appendix at the end of this journal.

Pass it Forward

Tools to empower your child's chakra development and help build their self-confidence

Understand who your child's friends are. Encourage relationships with those friends that strengthen and build your child's confidence.

Do core exercises with your child. This will help to build their will-centre.

Understand what fears your child has and why. Help them to move through their fears so that they grow beyond them.

Allow them to safely release any anger they may have, along with any other emotions they experience. If they are upset about a situation at school, allow them to get upset. Pound pillows, jump up and down, etc. Safely expressing anger shows children that it is a natural feeling; not one to be bottled up inside. Once they have expressed this emotion, ask them if they feel better and what are they feeling now. Explaining gently to our children that emotions are natural and part of being human has power beyond what we can imagine.

Encourage your child to journal. Journaling is a safe and expressive way to release emotions and help them naturally feel better. My daughter and I have 'journal time' together. We spend time each day writing in our own journals. Not only is this a way to spend time together, but it is also a way to heal individually.

The Heart Chakra

The heart chakra is considered the bridge between the lower and upper chakras. It begins its development between the ages of 22-28 and is associated with the color green. This transformational journey we are all on is a pathway into the heart centre. It is here that we discover the ideals of compassion, self-love, empathy, forgiveness, and non-judgement. When this chakra is energetically full, we feel great love for ourselves and the world. When this chakra is in depletion, we may experience loneliness, lack of empathy, or isolation. The heart holds the energy of our past relationships. It is here that we house a lot of pain and unhealed trauma. We may be holding the energy of hurt during our childhood, a recent breakup, the over-extension of energy to a parent or partner in need, or some other pain or hurt.

Every spiritual journey is a pathway back to opening our hearts. I remember being a child and my father telling me it was not okay to love yourself. He believed it was egotistical and not morally right. Yikes! Of course, he learned this from his parents. But, when you are taught this as a child you grow up believing that it is not acceptable to even like yourself, let alone love yourself. I have spent my whole life relearning that self-love is the greatest thing we can give ourselves.

Because the majority of us lack self-love, self-worth, and therefore confidence, we can get caught up in judgment, both about ourselves and what we think other people are saying about us. When our heart is filled with self-love, and we feel grounded and connected to who we are as individuals, the less these feelings of judgment rise up.

Referencing other people is something we talk about at length in my teacher training program and in my private counselling sessions. It's a big topic and it definitely is a practice in changing our thought process. Referencing other people means to be in constant thought about what we think other people may be thinking or saying about us. Most of the time, we stay small in order to by-pass any perceived judgment from others. We pass up the opportunity to be in the spotlight again and again because we are so afraid of failing in front of others.

The truth is, every time we move into thought and judgment about other people, we move into a contraction instead of an expansion. We shrivel up inside and the opportunity for freedom to be who we really are becomes limited.

In order to move away from fear about others and what they think of us we must notice our thoughts. We need to practice becoming an active witness to our thoughts. As in, "here comes that self-judgment again that says I'm not good enough to ask for that new position at work," or "here is that feeling of insecurity again, because I think people are talking about me".

Notice when the self judgment or the fear of what other people think of you arises. This begins a change in subconscious patterning. Replace the negative talk that you noticed. Repeat one of your favourite affirmations out loud or mentally over and over again until you notice a change in your body.

Moving away from self-judgment and judgment from other people is a practice. Our thoughts will always create our realities. If we decide to give energy into keeping negative self-talk as a permanent voice in our

lives, we will never move into self-love and confidence. If we stay trapped in worrying about what other people may think of us, we keep ourselves small and restrict our natural freedom to be who we are.

Keep in mind, we never really know what other people are saying or thinking about us. It is most often ourselves who are creating the energy behind these thoughts. I struggled with self-judgment and fear of what others thought of me for years. It was a constant and held me back from trying new things or moving into self-expression that felt natural, but at the same time too scary to even consider. With each day that passes, I grow more connected to myself. I trust my place in this world and know deep inside that there is nothing but infinite possibility for myself and every single one of us. It's a great space to be in.

The most important thing you can do to move away from this negative thought process is to become filled with self-love about who you are. You must feel a grounding into your centre. This journal is a journey back to wholeness. Its purpose is to establish the best relationship you can ever have with you.

Here is an exercise you can try when these old feelings of judgment or referencing other people arise for you.

Releasing Self-Judgment

1. Notice when these feelings are arising. Practice becoming an active witness to your thoughts. Write down in your journal whenever negative self-talk or the worry about what others think of you comes up.

2. Close your eyes and take several deep breaths. Connect to your breath.

3. Ask yourself, "Is this self-talk really true?"

4. Most often the answer is no. But if the answer that arises from your body is yes, then journal about why you think this is true about yourself. Let this answer be a conduit for your movement through your practices in this book to let that negativity go. This is just a falsehood that has been built through years of the same negative talk.

5. If the answer is a yes to the question of whether or not a person is talking about you, release the energy attached to it.

6. Inhale and think, "I am free to be exactly who I am with no restrictions".

7. Exhale and think, "I let go of judgment from myself and others".

8. Say to yourself, "I am perfect exactly as I am".

Simple, easy, and it really works. Remember; we have lived a certain way for a long period of time. We have trained ourselves to see our self and the world in a certain light. A lot of these exercises involve letting go of long held fears and stepping into the vast abyss of possibility.

When we begin to truly love ourselves, we step into the ownership of these actions:

Define Your Own Beauty. Don't wait until you lose weight, get the perfect hairstyle, or the perfect outfit to begin to realize self-love. Begin loving yourself by changing your focus to what is most important in your life. One of the ways I began to notice and appreciate my own beauty was deciding to focus on one thing I truly loved about myself. Maybe its your eyes, your hair, or your beautiful smile. Take some time to journal about what makes you unique. The feeling of true beauty begins when we let go of what we 'think' others believe about us and decide to love ourselves for everything that we are. When this feeling of self-love truly starts to cultivate within us, we begin to illuminate a radiant glow that is unmistakable.

Self-Care is Golden. Engage in the ritual of self-care. Take baths to cleanse your energy and begin anew. This is one of my most favourite rituals and I engage in baths at least twice a week. Become aware of your physical condition and do things to comfort yourself. Wait for the water to get warm before washing your hands. When you're tired after a long day at work, sit down and take a break before rushing into making dinner or doing other things around the house. Spend some time before bed creating a nighttime ritual that you can rely on to bring comfort and ease before falling asleep. This can be as simple as a breath practice. Breathe in for 4 counts, breathe out for 6 counts.. These are small ways you let yourself know that your comfort and well being are important.

Create Boundaries. This is probably one of the hardest things we can learn how to do. Often, we give so much of ourselves away on a daily basis, we don't even understand what a boundary is or how to create them. Consider where you can pull back in your life and take more time for you. Who drains your energy and who lifts it up? These simple little reflections will begin to shape the boundaries you need to invoke more self-love.

Anahata
The Heart Chakra

Meaning:
  -ana = un-
  -hata = struck/hurt/beaten
Colour: Green
Location: Center of Chest, Fourth Chakra
Element: Air
Mantra: YAM

I first began to chip away at the strong armour I had around my heart when I started my yoga practice. This coating was not unlike an armour of steel. The strange thing is, I didn't understand it was there until I began to tap into my body through my practice.

I was an extremely sensitive child and it was always easy for emotion to flow through me; until, one day, I decided this was not safe. When I was about 10-years-old my best friend and I were chased and beaten up by some neighbourhood kids. I came home hysterical. My dad, wanting to stop the crying, told me, "Don't be so sensitive. Don't cry. Don't be weak." As a kid, I equated this to protecting myself. To cry, to feel, to express emotion; this wasn't safe. My agreement then became to protect myself and my sensitivity. This, in turn, meant I closed off my heart chakra and began to coat it with a thick armour at which I am still, to this day, chipping away.

Naturally, we want to protect ourselves from feeling hurt and shame. We want to stay safe in the world, so when we an experience hurts us we often choose to close a part of us off to protect ourselves.

Take a moment to journal about your own experience with emotional expression, love, and trauma as a child.

Did your parents show signs of affection to each other and to you?

_____

_____

_____

_____

_____

_____

What is the earliest hurt you can remember? How did you process it? What did you decide to make yourself safe in the world?

_____

_____

_____

_____

_____

_____

_____

Take some time to process and journal about any other trauma you have experienced and still feel pain around.

_____

_____

_____

_____

_____

_____

_____

_____

_____

_____

Confidence Action Steps

Simple Ways to Open, Heal, and Clear your Heart Chakra

Go Forest Bathing. In Japan, forest bathing is known as shinrin-yoku, which means 'forest-bath'. This ritual is meant to be a meditative walk through the forest, allowing the trees, plants, and nature to open your senses and naturally heal you. Remembering that the heart chakra is green, you will find that when you spend mindful time in forest-like atmospheres, you are strengthening and healing this chakra.

Hug More! Choose to hug your family and friends more. Begin to radiate kindness out of your heart centre for all of those people that are truly special in your life. When we show love, we will naturally begin to receive more of it in return.

Mirror Talk. Look deep into your eyes in the mirror every day. Preferably in the morning and in the evening. Repeat three times, "I love you _____ (insert your name)". Beginning this exercise can be difficult at first, but eventually that feeling of being uncomfortable moves away and you start to form a deeper relationship with the person staring back at you in the mirror.

Repeat these affirmations, or the ones that have the most resonance for you every day:

> "I am fully open to giving love"
> "I am open to receiving love"
> "I forgive myself"
> "I love myself unconditionally"
> "I am open to fulfilling my heart's desires"
> "I am grateful for all of my blessings"

Close your eyes and bring in the image of your avatar. How do you see your avatar's heart space? Is it open and filled with self-love and compassion for others? Is she free of self-judgment? Write down the qualities you see in her that empower this chakra.

We are often the hardest on ourselves. Sometimes we don't even realize it, but the person we need to release from our judgement and criticism the most is ourselves. Write a loving letter to yourself here. Be free and open and explain the ways you have mistreated yourself or the things you have not yet forgiven yourself for. This is a great way to begin to open your heart.

_____

_____

_____

_____

_____

_____

_____

_____

_____

_____

_____

_____

_____

_____

_____

_____

_____

Write a letter to someone who you have not forgiven. Be free, clear, and open in the letter. Let all of your feelings go. When you feel ready, tear your letter out of the journal, light a small fire or a simple match, and burn the letter in a safe place. Watch the smoke leave the letter and breathe deeply, knowing that you have willingly released all ties to that person (or persons) and situation.

_____

_____

_____

_____

_____

_____

_____

_____

_____

_____

_____

_____

_____

_____

_____

_____

_____

_____

_____

Determine Your Boundaries

Begin to understand your own boundaries. Where do you allow others to dominate your energy and space? Who do you truly feel good around and who do you not feel good around? Begin to slowly make new parameters to protect your energy.

Everytime you let someone cross your personal boundaries in an unhealthy way, you are stepping away from self-love. Begin to heal this right here and now.

Pass it Forward

*Tools to empower your child's chakra development and
help build their self-confidence*

Hug More! Just as the confidence tip above lists, this is SO important for your child. Love is felt in many ways, one of which being warm, loving hugs. When your child experiences more affection from you, as well as observing it around them, they feel safe to open their heart chakra.

Encourage Forgiveness. Children will often have situations that come up in school that tests their own ability to live and let go. If we begin to teach them at a young age that it is ok to feel all of the emotions that come up around the events that hurt them, and then to forgive others and themselves, we are encouraging the act of self-love. We all make mistakes. It doesn't mean that everyone has to be our friend, but learning to let go of judgment and resentment around people is a pathway to freedom.

Encourage acts of self-love through self-care. Ask the question, what would make your heart sing today? What would fill you up with a warm feeling inside? When you hear the answers, make them come to life for your child. Imagine if you learned from a young age what to do to make your soul happy? Imagine if we all learned this… the world would be a different place.

The Throat Chakra

The cycle of the throat chakra is between the ages of 29-35 and is represented by the color blue. During this stage of development, we find our voice in the world and discover our comfort level with ourselves. This chakra is all about our self-expression, our life purpose, and our creativity.

The cycle of the throat chakra is between the ages of 29-35 and is represented by the color blue. During this stage of development, we find our voice in the world and discover our comfort level with ourselves. This chakra is all about our self-expression, our life purpose, and our creativity.

Doesn't it feel so good to say how you feel? For many of us, this is not easy; it certainly wasn't for me! Public speaking and offering my own opinion had been a fear of mine for most of my life.

I can still remember standing up to give a presentation in front of many senior people at a corporate company I onced worked for. I took one look at the people surrounding me, a look back at the screen behind me, and I totally blanked. I couldn't muster the confidence to even speak the words I had rehearsed. The reason this happened is because my throat chakra was suffering and I wasn't passionate about what I was about to speak of. In order for our throat chakra to be energetically positive, we need to speak, act, and exist from a place of inner truth.

Speaking my truth was always very hard for me; I learned from a young age that my voice didn't matter. For many children, this is a strong core belief which turns into an agreement that is supported by us over our lifetime; that is, unless we work to release it.

The majority of women that I coach, as well as many of my yoga students, suffer from a throat chakra deficiency. It usually begins when we are young and continues on in our growth into adulthood. When we suffer from blocks or energy depletion in this area of the energetic body, we may feel insecure, timid, or have a very low amount of self-confidence. It may also be difficult to truly hear what other people are trying to communicate to us and contribute to fear of speaking in front of others.

A deficiency here keeps our voices small in the world. When this chakra is blooming in full energetic capacity, we speak for what we feel is true and right for us. We are great communicators and take pleasure in sharing our views and opinions. We are also great listeners and make good friends. Our vision for ourself is clear and we feel confident enough to move to her.

Vishuddha
The Throat Chakra

Meaning:
    -vishuddha = purity
Colour: Blue
Location: Center of Neck, Fifth Chakra
Element: Space
Mantra: HAM

Take a deep breath into your lungs. Feel them fill up with fresh prana, life force, and renewed energy. Breathe out any resistance to the acceptance of this change in energy flowing through your body. This simple breath technique will begin to activate the light in your throat chakra.

Speaking our truth can be one of the most difficult things for us to accomplish. But when we begin to activate this practice of truth speaking, a whole new world opens up for us. Our speech gradually changes so that we can communicate our intentions clearly. We are able to consider situations in our life from different angles, we move out of hiding, and we step into self-confidence.

How creative are you? List some of the ways you can begin to spark your creativity.

_____

_____

_____

_____

_____

_____

_____

_____

_____

_____

Do you remember if it was easy or difficult to speak your truth as a child?

_____

_____

_____

_____

_____

_____

_____

How were your thoughts, feelings, and opinions valued? How has this affected you today?

_____

_____

_____

_____

_____

_____

_____

_____

_____

_____

_____

Where in your life do you need to start speaking your truth?

_____

_____

_____

_____

_____

_____

_____

_____

_____

Can you imagine what your life would look like if you opened up to infinite possibilities?

_____

_____

_____

_____

_____

_____

_____

_____

_____

_____

Confidence Action Steps

Simple Ways to Open, Heal, and Clear your Throat Chakra

Continue to journal your thoughts. This is important... and you are already doing it! Journaling is a way to process all the events that are happening to you.

Sing! That's right... sing! Sing in your car, sing at home, sing whenever it makes you feel good! I recently signed up for singing lessons and it is truly opening up my throat in ways I didn't believe possible.

Repeat these affirmations, or the one that speaks to you the most, every day:

Practice active listening. Really take some time to look into your friend, partner, son, or daughter's eyes and hear what they are saying. Ask them questions and show them you are right there with them in the experience.

Drink plenty of pure and alkalized water.

"My truth is powerful and I have a right to speak it"
"I communicate my feelings with ease"
"I have a right to speak all of my truths"
"I am grateful for all my blessings"
"I express myself creatively whenever I see fit"
"I am at Peace"

When we share those stories we've been scared to share, voicelessness loses it's wicked grasp ... - Jo Ann Fore

The Power of HA. I have been working with this mantra consistently over the past five years. It is my recipe for kick-ass chakra energy. This action alone has been such an important part of the healing of my root chakra, the freeing of my voice (throat chakra), and the strengthening of my will centre (solar plexus chakra). Chanting HA connects you to the earth and is representative of the energy of the sun. It brings a sense of empowerment that is undeniable!

As you begin to use this mantra, it may feel odd. This is simply a case of getting out of your comfort zone and trusting the process. Sometimes we don't even like the sound of our own voice and we have to just move past the judgment that arises through repetition. Try this every single morning and you will begin to feel empowered on a completely different level.

Stand with feet hip width apart and knees slightly bent. Inhale arms up to the sky and as you exhale, bring the elbows beside the body and say "HA," speaking from deep in your belly. Repeat, repeat, repeat! Practice for at least 3 minutes.

This is a solar mantra. It is meant to ignite our fire energy, passion, and determination to move forward in life. It also does a beautiful job of clearing our throat chakra.

Close your eyes and breathe into the image of your avatar. Is her throat chakra clear and bright? Does she trust her voice in the world and speak her truth? Is she filled with self-expression and freedom to be who she is? Journal about what qualities she holds that empower this chakra.

Just Say No

This week, say no to something you have wanted to say no to for a long time. Most of us grew up thinking that no is a word we can't say. We are taught to please everyone else but ourselves, until one day we are left asking ourselves, why do I feel so depleted?

No is a power word. It gives us the freedom to take back our energy from the things that we feel don't serve us. When we don't exercise the right to politely decline things, we are putting ourselves and our priorities on the back burner.

How many times have you said yes to something you later regretted? Take some time to consider this strong confidence action tip and understand where in your life you can start saying 'no'. When we begin to learn how to say no and communicate our thoughts and needs, we become naturally empowered.

Energy Class for the Heart and Throat Chakras

This class is designed to bring openness, healing, and transformation to your heart and throat chakras. We can carry a lot of built up tension, hurt, and repression in these areas of the body. Move into the resistance with ease and kindness. Let your breath become a medicinal wave of new energy that clears and heals everything. You are meant to be heard, seen, and loved.

*All energy classes can be found in the Energy Class Appendix at the end of this journal.

Pass it Forward

Tools to empower your child's chakra development and help build their self-confidence

Practice active listening with your child. Our body language, our facial expressions, and our overall willingness to be in conversation with our children (and everyone) is always felt. Every single one of us wants to be heard and when we feel that we aren't, it negatively affects our self-confidence.

Here are some ways to practice active listening:

- Maintain eye contact -

- Nod your head and smile -

- Provide feedback -

We practice active listening in my yoga teacher training program. Everyone is always amazed at how much they have forgotten about what it means to be in active conversation with someone. Living in a technological age, we are almost always distracted. This week, practice being an active listener with your child and talk to them about what that means. Listen and hear your child's words. Let them feel you with them in all of their sharing with you.

Encourage singing. I wish I had signed up for singing lessons as a child! Singing frees the soul. Everyone has a song vibrating in their soul. When our children learn from a young age that singing is beautiful and welcome, their throat chakra begins to naturally open. They realize that their own voice needs to be heard in the world.

Meditate with your child. Here is a simple visualization meditation for you and your child to practice:

- Sit with shoulders back and your spine straight.

- Inhale through your nose and exhale through your mouth.

- The throat chakra is tied to the colour blue. Begin to imagine that the throat area is filled with a beautiful blue glowing orb.

- Each time a breath comes into the body, imagine that the sphere of light becomes more brilliantly blue.

- Repeat for 2-5 minutes.

- A beautiful sense of calm and peace will surround you at the end of this meditation.

The Third Eye Chakra

The third eye chakra begins developing in full swing between the ages of 36 and 42. It is located between the brows, slightly above the bridge of the nose. When we activate this chakra we are strengthening the pineal gland, a pea-sized gland located in the vertebrate brain near the hypothalamus and pituitary gland. The color associated with this chakra is purple. Often when students tell me they see the colour purple in meditation or savasana, I assure them it is because their inner knowing is opening up.

This chakra is responsible for our inner knowing; it is the eye beyond our perception of ordinary sight. It is the home of our manifestations, thoughts, and perceptions. Those times when you have a feeling about something before it even happens or you think of a person and then the phone rings (I love it when this happens!)... this is your third eye chakra in action.

It is during this age that we are in full exploration of our spirituality and relationship to God and the universe. When we awaken the third eye we are very connected to our inner knowing. We are able to think clearly and develop our imagination easily. We trust in our opinions of others and can easily distinguish between the truth and falsehoods. Intuition flows easily.

When this chakra is blocked or underdeveloped, we may struggle with being close-minded, anxious, and even depressed. We don't trust our opinions of ourselves and others. Our intuition does not flow to us easily.

Our physical eyes see the material world, but our third eye connects us to our spiritual world. When we open this chakra, we begin to dissolve the illusion between self and spirit.

Ajna
The Third Eye Chakra

Meaning:
   -ajna = perceive/command/summoning
Colour: Indigo/Purple
Location: Center of Forehead, Sixth Chakra
Element: Light
Mantra: OM

When we begin to see each other through what the metaphysician calls the third eye, we begin to know each other on a level beyond what our physical eyes can see ...

- Marianne Williamson

Our inner world is more powerful than we realize. Lets face it, we humans are external in nature. We tend to give energy to the things in our life that we can physically see in front of us. Because we are not naturally inclined to activate our inner knowing and elevate our consciousness as we grow, the possibility of activating this power centre may seem daunting.

The truth is, it isn't complicated. Actively closing our eyes and taking moments of detachment from our surroundings throughout our day ignites the activation of the third eye centre. The more we do this, the more we begin to dissolve the veils between the physical and the spiritual worlds. The activation of this chakra allows our perceptions to increase; it helps us move away from staying caught in indecision and instead allows us to move forward because we 'just know' it to be the right choice. We naturally trust the signs we are given from our body and perceive the totality of life as oneness instead of separtness.

As children, we were all hyper sensitive to our inner knowing. We knew the right decisions to make and, for the most part, didn't ever question it. This unique connection is still inside of us. We just need to open the door of communication again.

Were you raised in a family that encouraged free thinking?

_____

_____

_____

Did your parents or caregivers value your insights?

_____

_____

_____

_____

_____

_____

_____

_____

Do you trust your inner knowing? How does your inner knowing show itself today?

_____

_____

_____

_____

_____

_____

_____

_____

_____

_____

_____

What was the earliest example you can remember of making a decision based on your gut instinct? What were the outcomes of this decision?

_____

_____

_____

_____

_____

_____

_____

How much time in reflection do you spend? Do you practice meditation or mindfulness?

_____

_____

_____

_____

_____

_____

_____

_____

_____

Confidence Action Steps

Simple Ways to Open, Heal, and Clear your Third Eye Chakra

Gaze at the Sun. Step outside, close your eyes, and let the light of the sun penetrate your third eye centre. Staring directly at the sun for the first few minutes of sunrise and sunset is said to activate the pineal gland (third eye centre). This is personally one of my favourite exercises.

Repeat these affirmations, or the one that resonates with you the most, every day:

> "My imagination is powerful and clear"
> "I am open to my own internal wisdom"
> "I create my reality"
> "I trust my intuition"

Keep a dream journal. Our dreams are filled with insight, even if we can't quite make sense of them. When we remember our dreams, we are working in unison with our souls. A great way to start remembering your dreams is to simply ask. Keep a specific dream journal on your night table and ask before you go to sleep to 'please remember my dreams'. When you wake up from a dream, be sure to write it down right away, because you most likely will forget about it once you get busy with everyday life. A dream journal keeps us connected to our spirit and begins a deeper connection with our inner knowing.

When we begin to see each other through what the metaphysician calls, the third eye, we begin to know each other on a level that is beyond what our physical eyes can see ...

- Marianne Williamson

The Practice of Trataka. Trataka is an ancient meditation practice that boosts concentration and memory, stills your mind, and begins to open the third eye. It helps us to tap into our own internal knowing and wisdom.

- Sit in meditation pose in front of a candle.

- Place the candle about an arms length away from you with the wick of the candle the same height as the chest (you don't want the candle any higher than this).

- Close your eyes and repeat a mantra that feels right to you, such as, "I am open to my own internal wisdom".

- Open your eyes and look at the candle without blinking. Concentrate on the upper part of the candle; the part that is the brightest.

- Close your eyes again. If the image of the candle appears within, gently concentrate on the image without causing any tension.

- Observe any thoughts that arise and let them go with your breath.

- Repeat three times.

This practice is a build. The time spent looking at the candle initially should only be 10-15 seconds, but can build up to a minute over a year of practice. This practice purifies the eyes, helps with sleeping and concentration, and builds your intuition. It can also be practiced with children.

Mindful Meditation to Open the Third Eye. Sit tall and close your eyes. Breathe deeply into your body, inhaling through the nose and exhaling through the mouth. When you feel settled in your physical form, gently bring your hands together in prayer and draw the thumbs to the third eye centre (in between and slightly above the eyebrows). Practice looking up to this chakra with your eyes closed.

- Begin to envision a ball of purple light rotating here in this centre.

- Let go of all thoughts and continue to breathe into this sphere of energy.

- Continue this practice for 2- 3 minutes.

As your practice deepens, it is in these moments that you can ask for answers to any questions you might have. Simply bring to your mind's eye to the question you have, breathe into the sphere of energy, and simply wait. Sometimes the answer will come quickly, other times you may get signs or hints over the next few days to move in a certain direction.

Strong Confidence Action Step

Speak to the Universe

This week, spend a few minutes in meditation and ask the universe a question. Patiently wait for the answer to arrive. It may come quickly, or it may take days. Watch for signs around you that are indications of the answer you have been waiting for. Tap into your body to feel what you are seeing.

Close your eyes and recall your avatar.

Does she smile back at you with a sense of inner knowing and connection? Is her third eye centre strong? Is she connected to herself on a deep internal level? What qualities does she hold that empower this chakra?

Pass it Forward

Tools to empower your child's chakra development and help build their self-confidence

Fresh Air & Fresh Sun. The more you can encourage your children to play outside and absorb the many benefits of the fresh air and the radiant sun, the more likely they will naturally strengthen this chakra centre.

Instinct Training. Look for daily examples of how to teach your child to trust her inner knowing. Ask about situations in school. How did they feel just prior to that event happening? Did they know something was going to happen before it actually did? I find there are many examples of children knowing much more than we think they do. More often than not, they know the answers to questions we are still thinking about! Praise them for tapping into insight. It will go far in the development of this energy centre.

Dress in Purple and LOVE their imaginary friends! Wearing the colour purple will help subconsciously strengthen this energy centre. My daughter wanted to paint her room purple recently and it looks beautiful! I also know it is helping her on a deeper level. The tea parties and hang outs with the imaginary friends are all good inner connection exercises too. It encourages imagination and tapping into an endless world within.

The Crown Chakra

This energy centre is the seat of our cosmic consciousness that we all carry. This is the discovery of your connection to your higher self and your connection to God or the universe. Its position is the very crown of the head. The development of this chakra is between the ages of 43-49 and its colour is violet or white.

When we are blocked in this chakra, we may be living in stressful environments or feel isolated and separate from everyone else. We also may suffer from a lack of life purpose and loneliness. When the Crown Chakra is balanced, we are easily able to connect and feel our spirituality and connection to God or the universe. You begin to see the world in a unified light. You may also crave a lot of time alone in order to cultivate and nurture this relationship. Feeling connected to our own wisdom and everyone around us at a cosmic level is a sign of a healthy Crown Chakra. Often times, when this chakra is deficient, it is due to unresolved trauma in childhood or the development of our limiting beliefs that we have agreed to our whole lives.

My own development of this chakra has really come just in the past few years. Even though as a child I felt deeply connected to source energy, that feeling drifted away from me as I grew through early adulthood and moved away from an inner practice. Now, I feel more

connected to source energy than ever before. I feel sure of my life purpose and the answers to questions I may have flow freely to me.

As you work on opening your Crown Chakra, you will begin to feel this amazing connection too.

The crown chakra is also referred to as 'the field'. It is difficult to truly define the cosmic nature of this powerful seventh chakra. It is truly beyond human comprehension.

What we do know is that when we are experiencing the opening of the crown chakra, we feel deep peace, joy, unification, and balance in all things. The positive activation of this centre allows us to release the ego effortlessly and realize that everything is connected. Like energetic vessels, we receive divine cosmic energy through the crown chakra and naturally give it away.

Sahasrara
The Crown Chakra

Meaning:
  -sahasrara = Lotus of the Thousand Petals
Colour: Violet, White
Location: Top of the Head, Seventh Chakra
Element: Wisdom
Mantra: OM, Silence

Here is a simple meditation you may use to open the crown chakra prior to journaling:

Meditation to Open the Crown Chakra

- Find a comfortable seat and breathe in and out until you feel yourself rest in your body.

- Begin to become the witness and observe your breath.

- Start to see a light at the root chakra. With your inhale, bring the light all the way up to the crown of the head and beyond, into the universe.

- With your exhale, see the same light travel back through the crown of the head, all the way down to the root chakra.

- Continue this meditation for 1- 3 minutes.

How connected to yourself and/or God or the Universe do you feel?

_____

_____

_____

_____

_____

_____

_____

_____

Do you remember your spiritual practices as a child? How did they make you feel?

_____

_____

_____

_____

_____

_____

_____

_____

What traumas do you remember experiencing as a child that may have blocked your connection to divine energy?

_____

_____

_____

_____

_____

_____

_____

_____

_____

_____

_____

What negative beliefs are causing you to feel cut off from source?

_____

_____

_____

_____

_____

_____

_____

_____

What are you ready to let go of?

_____

_____

_____

_____

_____

_____

_____

_____

_____

_____

Confidence Action Steps

Simple Ways to Open, Heal, and Clear your Crown Chakra

Meditate or practice visualization. Allow yourself to get quiet, observe the silence, and go within.

Repeat these affirmations every day, or the one you feel most connected too:

Connect and sit with a piece of nature you feel drawn to. Sit with your back against a tree and breathe through your heart, through your back, and into the tree. Send it love, light, and peaceful energy. Soon you will feel the tree returning this same energy to you.

"I am worthy of love from Divine energy"
"It is safe to receive Divine guidance"
"I am connected to my soul's purpose"
"I am connected to my higher self"
"I receive guidance from my angels, spirit guides, and benevolent energy"
"I am love"

When you touch the celestial in your heart, you will realize that the beauty of your soul is so pure, so vast and so devastating that you have no option but to merge with it. You have no option but to feel the rhythm of the universe in the rhythm of your heart ... - Amit Ray

Meditation to Deepen the Opening of the Crown Chakra

- Sit comfortably and breath deeply. Feel your feet firmly on the floor, palms open, and forearms resting gently on your thighs.

- Feel yourself release and let go of any worldly problems, issues, or concerns.

- Let your forehead soften, let your shoulders drop down, soften your hips.

- Breathe deeply three times through the nose and then exhale through the mouth.

- Begin to envision a beautiful lotus flower above the crown of the head.

- With each inhale, see the lotus flower becoming larger. With each exhale, feel any resistance you carry in your body leave with a light grey mist.

- Continue this for at least one minute.

- Begin to see the lotus flower pour violet coloured energy into the crown of your head and fill your whole body.

- Continue this practice until you feel you are filled with this beautiful light.

- Breathe in, breathe out.

- Open your eyes and experience the difference in your body, mind, and spirit.

Breathe into the image of your avatar.

Does she emit the energy of connection to the universe? Is there peace inside of her? How connected is she to source energy or God? Contemplate what the openness of this chakra means to you and add it to your idealized self image.

Simplify

When we live in clutter; a messy desk, a busy kitchen, a cluttered bathroom; we live in the same clutter in our minds. Slowly but surely, make your way through your home and simplify your surroundings. This provides clarity in your mind, body, and spirit and allows for new space to create the life we want to live.

Pass it Forward

Tools to empower your child's chakra development and
help build their self-confidence

Create a spiritual practice for you and your child. At bedtime, my daughter and I say a prayer and bless and give thanks for everyone in our life. This may seem simple, but it births the beginning of a ritual for your child into their own spirituality.

Practice mindfulness with your child. Mindfulness can be as simple as picking up a rock and inspecting the different crevices and bumps with curiosity. Ask your child to tell a story around what they see in the rock or peice of nature that she or he is drawn too. This creates present day feelings and steps away from mind chatter.

Colours! Choose to wear or surround your child with the color violet or white. This is a simple way to strengthen their crown chakra.

Body Reconnection Meditation

Deep breaths...

Whether you took your time exploring each chakra or have skipped ahead to this part of your journal, it is where you are meant to be, and it is perfect.

Any of the meditations, exercises, or energy routines provided in this section of the journal will continue to bring you into a new state of balance, creation, and confidence.

Remember: it is so important to do one thing a day to help reconnect you to your inner essence. This is my 'must do' tip in order to change your current reality into the idealized image of everything you envision yourself encompassing.

This is a body reconnection meditation I created to help seal and reinforce the power of connecting. It can be practiced multiple times a day. The more we practice anything that lifts our vibration, the more we have no choice but to keep elevating ourselves to a new way of being in the world.

- Sit up nice and tall, supporting yourself if you need too.
- Breathe in through your nose and exhale out through your mouth, giving up all thoughts, stresses, and anything that keeps you from the now.
- Using the first finger and thumb of the right hand, lightly squeeze the nail beds of each finger of the left hand and repeat for each finger: "I am in ideal health," "I am in ideal balance," "I am my ideal weight," and "I am bathing in pure radiance, energy and vitality".
- Continue this meditation for 2-3 minutes every single day.
- You will notice your self-confidence building each time.

Part Two

My Powerful Mind

The Creator of my World

We are never really empowered to grow; we are conditioned to stay the same.

To my limiting beliefs…
Thank you.
You have kept me safe.

Our limiting beliefs are any thoughts that restrict our lives in some way. We adopt them when we are small because we feel they keep us safe. Then we look for evidence to support our limiting beliefs and keep them alive as we grow, even when they no longer support or protect us.

As we mature from a child into an adult, we are told that certain things are considered good behaviour while others are labelled as bad behaviour. This can show up in many different ways. Perhaps we take more cookies than we were offered and are called selfish or greedy by our parents. Or maybe we offer our opinion on something without being asked and are called a know-it-all by our friends. All of these small experiences reek havoc on our self-esteem. We classify our behaviour as 'bad' or 'wrong' and make decisions about the world based on these experiences. They shape who we are today.

Based on our specific experiences, our limiting beliefs might sound something like this:

"It's not safe to want more than your share."
"It's not safe to speak my truth."

There are countless limiting beliefs that we adopt as we grow. Most of them are locked in our subconscious and we have no idea we are living with such restriction.

Here are some common limiting beliefs people attach to themselves:

I'm too old.

I'm too young.

I'm too poor. I lack money and resources.

Money is the root of all evil.

Rich people hold all the good cards.

I can never fail.

I must overachieve.

I'm too fat or too skinny; too tall or too short.

I'm too far gone to start taking care of my body now.

There is never enough time.

I'll never be happy.

People won't like the real me.

Others are in my way.

One day I will change.

Change is too hard.

I'm powerless.

I'm a mess; it's hopeless.

I'm not smart enough.

I'm not popular enough.

I'm not connected enough.

I'm not strong enough.

I'm not good enough.

I'm too much.

I'm not enough.

Take a deep breath and consider whether any of these feel true to you. Circle the beliefs you relate to and would like to address.

At some point in time, a situation (or rather, many situations) in our life happens and we adopt a limiting belief that we subconsciously decide is true and keeps us safe in the world. From then on, we carry it with us wherever we go. We begin clamming up when our opinion differs from others, or we never strive for more than we have for fear of overstepping an invisible boundary we created long ago.

The result of all these limiting beliefs? An equally limited life. A life that hides our truth and dumbs down our creativity, our connection to our essence, and our self-confidence in all of our capabilities.

As my own yoga practice deepened, I was reminded of instances in my life that were painful. One day, I was practicing pigeon pose and I remembered being rejected by certain girls at school. This instance of my life left me feeling lacking and not good enough. Not being good enough became my limiting belief and I carried it with me until I began deepening my connection to my physical body. It wasn't until this yoga class and this particular pose that a memory locked deep inside of me came up for release.

Your physical body is a storehouse of unprocessed emotions.

Everything we have ever experienced in our lives that has not been acknowledged, felt, and moved through still remains in our bodies. When we hold deep poses in yoga, these memories and emotions will sometimes surface. For me, it was clear that these memories were coming up for a reason and that I needed to work on clearing them in order to become free and grow into the person I was meant to be.

I have worked with numerous clients who didn't believe they had any memories of their childhood. Trust me; those memories are all still there! Once my clients and I began to address the physical body and directly acknowledge the feelings they were presently working with, memories arose. If we are to be free, confident, and empowered, we have to accept and process the experiences that have happened to us along the way.

Here are some more of my own limiting beliefs that I have worked through:

"The world is not safe".
"Don't get too excited; you may lose everything".
"Don't speak unless spoken too".
"Being sensitive and showing vulnerability is wrong".

The world conditions us to label ourselves as 'good' or 'bad' on a daily basis and we in turn adopt new behaviours to fit into society's standards. This leads us to form a belief system and a way of adapting in the world in order to keep ourselves safe.

When we begin to work through our limiting beliefs, we create a freedom inside of us we never believed possible. Remember, everything takes up space. Every unresolved incident leaves a residue inside of our bodies, waiting to be resolved. Our spirit wants to heal these events. Deep down inside, we yearn to be free of them.

Explore the Inner You... Limiting Beliefs Exploration

What are some of your limiting beliefs?

What are you ready to let go of?

Can you remember a situation as a child where you felt unsafe that may have caused you to see the world differently?

_____

_____

_____

_____

_____

_____

_____

_____

_____

_____

_____

_____

_____

_____

_____

_____

If we can see past preconceived limitations, then the possibilities are endless ... - Amy Purdy

The River of My Emotions

The Guest House

This being human is a guest house.

Every morning a new arrival.

A joy, a depression, a meanness,

some momentary awareness comes

as an unexpected visitor.

Welcome and entertain them all!

Even if they are a crowd of sorrows,

who violently sweep your house

empty of its furniture,

still, treat each guest honourably.

He may be clearing you out

for some new delight.

The dark thought, the shame, the malice.

meet them at the door laughing and invite them in.

Be grateful for whatever comes.

Because each has been sent

as a guide from beyond.

Rumi

Our emotions are part of who we are. Like the flowing water, they run through us every second of every day. As children, most of us were not taught how to properly accept and feel our emotions. Instead, we were conditioned to express what society told us was acceptable instead of what felt natural or innately correct.

As we journal and open the door to understanding our limiting beliefs, old held-back emotions may naturally come to the surface. You may have the urge to cry or express anger around an old issue that you haven't thought about in years. Fabulous! This is all GREAT stuff. This is what we want!! It means you are actively letting go of the past and freeing space for stepping into the greatness of who you truly are.

The Guest House by Rumi is one of my favourite poems. It relays that part of our humanity is understanding that every experience we encounter is valuable. Every emotion we feel is valid, no matter what shows up. When we experience moments of shame, guilt, anger, or sadness, they are meant to be felt and moved through. Each one is the opening to a new awareness.

Most of us grow up without understanding how to fully feel. As children, many of us held back our darker feelings for fear of shame from our parents; we didn't feel safe expressing the sadness, anger, or other dark emotions we experienced.

Do any of these statements sound familiar?

"Don't get angry… be happy!"
"Nice girls don't get mad."
"If you want to be sad, do it elsewhere."
"You're overreacting."

We all grow up giving a lot of meaning to our external environment. We don't trust in that which we cannot see, so when we feel dark emotions like sadness or anger, we try to dismiss it and bury it away. But we don't fully understand the power of this dismissal. Emotions that are dismissed and repressed come back to haunt us later in life. They are the reason we get overly angry at something that seemingly shouldn't be so disturbing. We are still upset about the time our mom or dad blamed us for something that wasn't our fault. That very emotion is waiting to get out of the body, so our anger over everyday situations may be amplified. We may hold back the desire to advance forward in different areas of our lives because the fear of failure far outweighs the risk it would take to put ourselves out there. It's not a nice way to live this one great life.

Most of my students, especially in yoga teacher training, are shocked when they realize how many untapped emotions they have been holding onto. When we work through classes and energetic cleansing techniques, the body begins to feel safe enough to release what has been trapped. When we learn to bring to the surface the parts of ourselves that are disowned, we become a more complete version of ourselves. We become confident in recognizing that our feelings are all valid; that they are all part of our experience as an individual on the journey to becoming whole.

The body holds everything for us. Every unprocessed emotion or thought is like a beach ball that simply waits inside of us to be let go. The purpose of this section of the book is to tap into and feel these hidden emotions. No doubt, a lot of things must have arisen in your work to open your body and free it from restriction in the last section. The sacred energy pathways of your chakras have been opened, nourished, and fed. Now it is important to let go of anything that you feel you haven't quite released. Let's tap into the little child inside of you that wants to be heard; let's greet her with love, forgiveness, and new light.

Inner Child Meditation. The inner child is the part of ourselves that has been influenced by our impressions of the physical world. For your inner child to come to the surface, they need to feel safe. They need to feel that you are there for them.

Find a safe, secure place in which you won't be disturbed. Keep this journal close by. Follow these steps:

- Close your eyes and breathe deeply.

- Let every exhale release any hesitations, stress, or negative thoughts.

- Imagine yourself in nature. Your most favourite outdoor place. As you look around, notice the smells, the sounds, and the feelings. I always see myself on a beautiful sandy beach. If you don't see anything, it's totally okay, simply feel the feeling of where you are.

- Wherever your soul has taken you, feel the warm sun on your face as you gaze towards it. Feel your breath softly releasing anything that you have carried with you into this moment.

- Gently turn towards your left and notice a small child walking towards you.

- As they approach, turn to greet them. When they arrive, gently take their hands.

- Notice that this is your 4-year-old self (it may be younger or older).

- Take your child self in. See their emotions and energy expression. What are they showing you? How are they feeling?

- Start to beam love into them from your heart, through your arms, from your hands, and into their arms and upwards towards their heart. Continue to do this as long as you feel called to. Allow your inner child to feel loving acceptance for everything that they are.

- When your child self feels secure, ask them if there is anything you need to know or release.

- Journal about what you saw, what you experienced, and anything your inner child had to offer you.

This inner child meditation can, and should, be practiced often. You want to continue to tap into the emotional side of your energetic body so that it feels safe to release anything that has been repressed.

Sometimes it is hard for us to visualize these images. Keep trying and if you can't see anything, focus on the energy of your heart centre and notice the difference in its feeling when you are tapping into this mediation.

Take some time to journal about the images and experiences that came up for you during this meditation. If you struggled to visualize the images, journal instead about the feelings and inner changes that you observed throughout the meditation.

What did your inner child look like?

_____

_____

_____

_____

_____

How did it feel to offer them love and acceptance?

_____

_____

_____

_____

_____

_____

_____

_____

What feelings came up for you that need to be released?

_____

_____

_____

_____

_____

_____

_____

_____

_____

_____

_____

_____

_____

_____

_____

_____

_____

_____

Caring for your inner child has a powerful and surprisingly quick result:
Do it and the child heals ... - Martha Beck

Tapping: An Exercise of Emotional Freedom

I used to think to myself, "I wish I could help make a larger shift in my students' lives". For years, I was teaching yoga to the same group of students. They loved the practice, but there seemed to be a missing link: the freedom to express emotion. "How do we do this safely?" I used to wonder.

When you ask, the universe does answer! Shortly after this pondering, I was introduced to something called Emotional Freedom Technique; a simple and effective way to release trapped emotions in the body. I was so taken with this practice that I went on to get my certification in the field. It is now one of the primary ways I work to bring emotional freedom to my clients' lives.

Tapping is a powerful, holistic healing technique that has been proven to resolve a range of afflictions from stress, addictions, limiting beliefs, anxiety, and fears. It is based upon the combined principles of ancient Chinese acupressure and modern psychology. Using the fingertips to tap on specific meridian points of the body while bringing to mind a dark emotion naturally calms the nervous system and rewires the brain to respond in healthier ways.

Quite simply and speaking from my own personal experience, tapping works.

Tapping to Release Emotions. Take a moment and close your eyes. Consider what you want to release. What emotions came up in the inner child meditation? Or what has come up throughout the body section of the journal that you want to work on? What situations still have an effect on you today? There will be many, but for the purpose of this section, I will use one example of an emotion that will need to be released by many of us: shame.

1) Think about the situation that you would like to release. Rate the shame attached to it from 1 to 10 (10 being extreme and 1 being no shame at all). Write it down in your journal or follow the prompts on pages 114-115.

2) Compose a setup statement. You want to acknowledge the problem that has to be dealt with, followed by an unconditional affirmation of yourself as a person. For example:

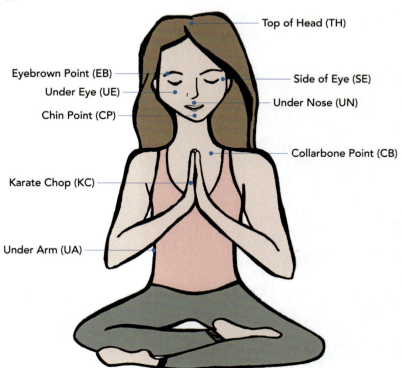

"Even though I still feel this shame, I deeply and completely accept myself".

OR

"Even though I feel shame around (insert your situation here), I deeply and completely love and accept myself".

3) Begin tapping using the following method:

- With four fingers of one hand, begin tapping the Karate Chop (KC) point on your other hand. The Karate Chop (KC) point is on the outer edge of the hand, on the opposite side from the thumb.

- Repeat the setup statement three times aloud while simultaneously tapping the KC point. Now take 3-5 deep breaths, in through the nose and out through the mouth.

- Using the same hand, but only two fingers, continue to tap five-to-seven times on each remaining eight points listed below. As you tap on each point say, "my shame," to remind yourself of the emotion you are releasing.

Eyebrow Point (EB) Where the eyebrows begin, close to the bridge of the nose

Side of Eye (SE) On the bone directly along the outside of each eye.

Under Eye (UE) On the bone directly under each eye.

Under Nose (UN) The area directly beneath the nose and above the upper lip.

Chin Point (CP) This is the area just below your bottom lip and above the chin, right in the crease.

Collarbone Point (CB) Starting from where your collar bones meet in the centre, go down an inch and out an inch on each side.

Under Arm (UA) On your ribcage, about four inches beneath the armpit.

Top of Head (TH) Directly on the crown of your head.

- Take another deep breath.

4) This completes one round of tapping. Think about the issue again and the emotion of shame that is attached to it (or whichever emotion you chose to work on).

5) Take a few deep breaths, close your eyes, and re-connect to that situation. Do you have the same rise or emotional reaction in your body?

6) Rate the feeling from 1- 10 again. Did you notice a change? Sometimes we have to tap several rounds before the emotion reaches neutral in the body. When it moves to this level, you have successfully acknowledged, felt, and released an old emotion.

Often times, when we tap on one emotion, another memory will come to surface with a separate feeling that needs to be released. Keep a journal close to you and remember to write down everything that comes up around each tapping session.

This section of the book is an opportunity for you to get clearer in your mind, body, and heart. It is a chance for you to do your own self work and healing around old issues. It is meant to be a process, so please go easy on yourself. Take the time to set up your environment in a way that supports this deep healing work.

Explore the Inner You... Emotions I Wish to Release

1) Describe the situation you are reflecting upon.

2) What emotions come up? Choose one you would like to focus on and release.

3) Rate the strength of this emotion from 1-10 (10 being strong and 1 being neutral).

4) Complete the tapping exercise found on pages 112-113.

5) Reflect on the situation once again. Now rate the strength of the emotion you have been working with.

_____

_____

_____

_____

_____

_____

_____

_____

_____

_____

_____

_____

_____

_____

_____

_____

_____

In order to move on, you must understand why you felt what you did and why you no longer need to feel it ... - Mitch Albom

A Few Thoughts on Anger. Anger is a hidden emotion that most of us suppress on a daily basis. As with every other emotion, anger is not something that we are taught how to properly move through. Society teaches us that anger is something to be overcome, not something to embrace. We are taught that it is poison and that we must put it aside and simply substitute in the lighter feelings of joy, happiness, or laughter.

As a child I was not permitted to get angry. I was taught that it was not a safe thing to express. Girls didn't get angry, and my mother sure didn't, so why would it be safe for me to do so?

When I entered into teaching yoga, I quickly gained a reputation for being a tough yoga teacher. I developed and taught my own 'yoga boot camps' which were physically and emotionally demanding on all of my students. Years later, I came to understand that I was using this class as an outlet to express my anger. I was rinsing out the trapped emotion that had been stuck in my body for so long. Nevertheless, the class was extremely popular! Turns out it wasn't just me who needed to move my anger; the students wanted to share in that as well.

Let's face it; if we get down and dirty with ourselves, we are going to dig up an anger list a mile long. It could be as deep as your 4th grade teacher embarrassing you to your father forbidding you to date until you were a certain age (that's one of mine) to anything in between.

Holding on to anger can be likened to a tight rope that connects you to the person with whom you are angry. This tight rope traps energy and keeps us emotionally and spiritually stuck. Trust me, there is a world of freedom when we move through our anger and let our old grievances go.

The key to acknowledging and expressing our anger properly is the secret to releasing every cell of toxicity in our bodies. A simple and effective way to begin this process is to Rant. Ranting is simply tapping on all of the same points of the body as above while expressing your frustrated and anger-like feelings to the person you feel anger towards.

I am so happy to share this with you; it is another one of my favourite things to teach my students and personal clients.

Ranting Practice. Take a few moments here and breathe deeply.

Go on a journey into your past and think about the situations and people that you still might be angry with and list them all here:

The people and situations from the past I still hold anger towards are…

_____

_____

_____

_____

_____

_____

When you have arrived at a situation that you would like to tap through, take a moment, close your eyes and go back to that specific incident. How angry do you feel just thinking about it? Rate your anger from 1- 10 (10 being the most angry you could be) before beginning the below sequence.

On a scale of 1-10, my anger about this situation is currently: _____

Tap on the karate chop point of the hand while saying each of these statements:

- Even though I feel really frustrated with _____, I deeply and completely love and accept myself.

- Even though I feel so frustrated with_____, I realize my anger is not a fault.

- Even though I feel angry and frustrated with_____, I know I am able to free myself from this emotion.

Now begin to talk to the person like they are sitting in the chair in front of you while tapping. Use the first and second finger of one hand to tap on each of the below points and repeat the associated sentence.

Eyebrow: I feel so angry with you, _____.

Side of the Eye: I want to scream; I feel so frustrated.

Under the Eye: I feel this anger in my body and I have been holding onto it for so long.

Under the Nose: And I know it is really hurting me.

Chin Point: I can't believe you did that to me.

Collarbone: You are a selfish, narcissistic jerk.

Under the Arm: And I have a right to be frustrated.

Top of the Head: So I'm going to let myself feel this frustration right now.

Eyebrow: I've been told so many times I shouldn't feel the way I feel.

Side of the Eye: But this time, I'm going to really indulge these feelings while I tap.

Under the Eye: It's high time I honoured my feelings.

Under the Nose: What if, by allowing myself to really feel these feelings, I'm better able to release them?

Chin Point: What if, in doing so, I can really free myself from these frustrated feelings?

Collarbone: What if this is what feelings are meant to do; just move through me by allowing them?

Under the Arm: This is different thinking for me.

Top of the Head: What if, by allowing myself to fully feel my feelings on my own, I'll be able to let them go and really free myself and not hurt anyone in the process?

Take several deep breaths.

Now rate your intensity of the anger again... has it changed?

On a scale of 1-10, my anger about this situation is currently: _____

If it hasn't quite moved, continue to rant, rant, rant!! Express what you need to express until you feel neutral about the situation. Once you reach neutrality, you have cleared this from your emotional, physical, and spiritual form. You have successfully created new space.

Beginning today, and forever more, continue to work towards accepting your feelings. The best way to do this is to continue to let them move through you with the practice of tapping and ranting. The more you tap, the more things will come up that need to be released. Some of these things will seem simple and you may not even be sure why it's come up in memory, but nevertheless, they all are taking up space inside of you.

When we are filled with regret, sadness, grief, shame, and anger, we are dwelling in low lying vibrational living that prevents us from moving forward in life.

To feel confident means to accept ALL of you. It means understanding that things happen and that they are all part of this great experience that is your journey in life. When we can accept, forgive, and see the value of the lesson in each experience, then we are moving forward full speed towards becoming the greatest version of who we can be. Nothing holds us back.

Take some time here to journal about the incidents that you are tapping around, how you feel about them now, and what the lesson was that they taught you.

How do you feel about the incidents you were Ranting around now that your rant is complete?

_____

_____

_____

_____

_____

_____

What lessons can you see that these experiences of anger taught you?

_____

_____

_____

_____

_____

_____

_____

Confidence Action Steps

Simple Ways to Empower Yourself to Feel Freely

Make a commitment to take time each day to express emotions that have arisen. If you can't do it in the moment, make a note and do it later in the day. I even tap in my car!

Repeat these affirmations every day, or the one that speaks to you the most:

> "My feelings flow through me"
> "All of my feelings are valid"
> "I love every single part of me"

Anger exists to move us into action, whenever action is needed to protect our boundaries our sense of self, or whatever we consider to be "ours" ... - Jessica Moore

Pass it Forward

Tools to empower your child to feel and release their emotions

We change the world by instilling what we learn in the hearts of our children. An easy way to help kids move through emotions is to introduce tapping to them. It takes a child far less time to tap through something that came up for them that was hurtful. Children respond really well to tapping. This practice validates their feelings and instills a new skill that they can take with them for the rest of their lives!

Part Three

My Beloved Spirit

The Soul Behind my Eyes

As a child, I was deeply connected to my essence, or what I knew to be my spirit, through prayer. There was always a part of me that felt deeply connected to Source energy. I would notice a difference in how I felt if I missed small prayers at night or my regular "mini conversations" with God.

My family was not extremely religious. I was raised Catholic and went to a Catholic school, but we did not 'follow all the rules' per se. Prayer was my own thing; I engaged in it almost nightly from the time I was about 6-years-old. I remember feeling angels around me when I would ask for guidance or to be protected. This connection felt very real, grounding, and true.

As I grew older, my connection to Spirit lessened. I lost my ritual of prayer and I consequently became more disconnected from that solid place of connection inside of me.

I began to hang out with the wrong crowds, ended up in jobs that paid well but didn't make me happy, and entered into the wrong relationships. This karmic period, as I like to call it, lasted about 13 years.

I remember being at work one day, frustrated with where I was in life, and simply asking the universe to show me; to guide me to where I needed to go or show me what I needed to see to serve who I really was. Shortly after this, I miraculously saw an ad in a local paper for a yoga class. My participation in that class changed my entire life. It wasn't the teacher or the studio; it was the connection I felt to my breath, my body, and then my soul. I knew instantly that I had found what I was searching for.

This journal is a play-by-play account of the steps I took to become connected to my most authentic self. It is a recreation of how I grew to feel confident, grounded, and secure in who I am. Our connection to our spirit is always there. In fact, it is here right now, waiting for you to accept it. It is in every single practice of this journal. Your spirit is the perfect you. You are already perfect just as you are; the key is simply peeling back the layers of self-doubt, old agreements, and limiting beliefs and deciding to see, breathe, and live in your preferred vibration.

What is your preferred vibration? Happiness? Joy? Peace? Empowerment? Throughout the "My Amazing Body" section of this journal, you were invited to continue creating your avatar at the end of each chapter. What does she look like now? When you close your eyes and see this radiant image of you, what are all of the feelings that she encompasses?

One of the ways we can continue to live in the preferred vibration of our choosing; for example, the feeling of being confident; is to develop our own daily rituals that bring us back to this avatar... back to who we really are.

I would not be who I am today if I did not embrace my own daily rituals to connect to my spirit. Sometimes, I am able to spend only five minutes practicing; other days I have the time to commit an entire hour to my practice. But the days that I cannot engage at all are the days I am at my worst. I feel disconnected, unbalanced, and frazzled.

I always tell my clients and students that if you begin to commit to five minutes each day to breathe, meditate, and connect to your essence in whatever way feels right to you, then that is all you need to change the entire vibration of your day. This time we spend connecting to ourselves is the building of our relationship with our spirit. It creates the strengthening of our internal knowing of who we really are and releases the attachment to the external world around us.

Remember, any of the confidence action steps, tips, affirmations, practices, and energy classes taught in this journal are steps on the path to connect to your spirit. Choosing one simple thing each day will begin to harvest your soul connection and the inherent confidence you are searching for.

I want to share with you some of my favourite breath techniques. These are simple techniques that you can do every day to continue to strengthen your bond with Spirit.

Rituals to Connect to Spirit Throughout Your Day

Morning Breath to Start the Day. This is an easy practice I always turn to first thing in the morning. You can do this lying down or sitting up; whichever feels right for you.

- Upon opening your eyes in the morning, place one hand on our belly and the other hand on your heart.

- Take a deep breath in and feel your belly rise on the inhale. As you exhale, feel the belly gently return back to the spine.

- Continue this for several breaths and connect to your body's energy today.

- Begin to exhale out through your mouth any feelings of despair, stress, or self-doubt that may be coming to the surface.

- Begin to call to mind the one way you wish to feel today. Is it confident, happy, joyful, or peaceful? Something else?

- With every inhale, breathe in this feeling. With every exhale, let go of the resistance to moving into this new vibration.

Midday Breath for Stress-Relief. Remember how I mentioned I used to work in jobs that didn't serve me? I used to practice this breath routine to help ease the stress I would feel in my body while at those jobs. It's simple and it works.

- Close your eyes if you can and begin to take long, deep breaths in through the nose and out through the mouth.

- When you feel a bit more settled, start to imagine that the in breath is flooding your body with the essence of peace and calming energy. I personally love to give it a colour. You may see blue, yellow, or white. It doesn't matter what colour shows up in your awareness; trust that it is the healing colour your body needs.

- Continue to breathe in, imaging the colour is filling you up from your toes all the way up to the crown of your head.

- When you feel complete, take a few moments and notice the difference in your body's energy.

Evening Breath to End the Day. It's the end of the day. A lot has happened, no doubt! Often our trouble with falling asleep at night comes from not understanding how to quiet the thoughts that continuously flow in our minds. Here is a simple practice I often use to close out the energy of my day.

- Sit or lie down comfortably.
- Begin to take deep breaths in through your nose and out through your mouth.
- With each deep inhale, feel as though you are drawing in a healing energy. With every full exhale, feel as though you are surrendering the tension in your body a bit more.
- Continue until you feel more relaxed.
- Begin to count silently to 4 as you inhale and as you exhale count to 6. Repeat this practice for 1- 2 minutes.
- A mantra to add in to this breath routine is 'I am relaxed' on the inhale and 'I let go' on the exhale.

Connecting with Spirit Exploration

How did these breath practices feel? Did they bring about a sense of calm?

List some things you have learned throughout this journal that you can do each day to connect to your spirit.

Pass it Forward

Tools to help your child connect to their spirit

Our children need to learn to embrace their breath and use it as a tool to stay connected to their spirit. Any of these breath techniques above can be used for your child.

When my daughter experiences stress, we engage in big inhales and big exhales (together) to let go of whatever is causing the imbalance. We continue this until she feels balanced and her breath naturally takes on an even pace.

These techniques work quickly with children. The feeling is acknowledged, accepted, and gently moved through the body. Before you know it, they are on to the next exciting thing!

Returning to Your Avatar

As we move along the path to transformation, one of the most important things we have to keep in our awareness is our vision of our idealized self. The person we see ourselves to be, without judgment or restrictions of any kind; the YOU without any limits.

Throughout the pages of this journal, you were prompted to continue creating and adding to the great vision of yourself that you are stepping into. These prompts were clues and hints along the way to help you decide which qualities you needed to embrace to help balance your energetic system and become the greatest version of you.

Use the space here to define all of the qualites your avatar now holds. Sketch, create, and build her vibration, her preferred way of feeling, her environment, even her role in the world! Close your eyes for a few moments. Breath deeply. What do you see?

_____

_____

_____

_____

_____

_____

_____

_____

_____

Use this space to draw, sketch, or design your avatar. Be as detailed as possible. Explore what she looks like, where she is, and what she's doing in the image.

When something ends, something new begins...

When we are spiritually healthy, we are living in-line with our truest self. As you begin to balance the energy of your chakras and work with the transformative actions in this journal, your relationship with your spirit will naturally thrive and deepen.

It is important to keep in mind that the more we practice living in our preferred state of being, the less our old, fearful, limiting self will keep appearing. Remember: you have lived a certain way for a long period of time. It takes patience to change your habits, your thoughts, your reactions, and your belief systems. And remember: anything you desire is possible.

We create the life we are living. Anything you wish to be or become is right in front of you. Your best dream for yourself is waiting for you to move towards her. Begin to make the avatar you have created the reference point for your new self. Every single day, look at the avatar and see yourself as inhabiting all of the qualities, feelings, and dreams that she represents.

Remember, not everyday is the same. Some days it will feel easy to slip back into an old way of being. Don't be hard on yourself. We are human and allowed to fall off the tracks once in a while. If this happens, take a deep breath, let it go, journal about it, and start again.

The greatest project you'll ever take on is you. And once you accept this and take on the mission, your soul will begin to feel fed in ways it hasn't ever before. This feeling is indescribable. Your vibration will begin to lift and you will start to assume a beautiful new radiance. The people in your life will notice this about you and will want to be around you; to feel the same way.

When we heal, everyone heals.

Remember...

YOU ARE AMAZING.
YOU ARE LIMITLESS.
YOU ARE CONFIDENT.

Thank you for taking this journey with me and for trusting me along the path. It is a great honour to teach others the things I have learned myself.

With Love,

Carol Anne Baxter

Energy Classes for Confidence

Energy Class for the Root Chakra

1) Connecting Pose (Meditation Stance)

Sitting on a bolster or a pillow, or maybe just on the floor, find easy pose with one shin crossed in front of the other. Take a grounding posture with your palms face down on your knees.

Take some time here and just breathe. Feel your belly expand on the inhale and retract on the exhale. Connect to the energy of your feet, your legs, your sacrum, hips, belly, chest, shoulders, neck, and crown of the head. Using your breath, travel the fingers of your mind from your toes all the way up to the crown of the head, over and over again until you feel very connected to your body.

All that matters right now is you...
Let the rest of the world go...

2) Seated Spinal Flex

Remaining in easy pose, remove any props you have supporting you and ease your way onto the ground. Bring your hands to your shins or ankles and breathe in, flexing the lower spine forward. Then breath out and flex backward.

Keep your head level and your chin in a neutral position. Keep the breath traveling through the nose. Close your eyes and continue for 3 minutes, moving with the breath.

This exercise works on the first chakra, releasing tension and moving energy up the spine. You will instantly notice a calmer feeling from doing this one exercise. It is one of my favourites!

3) Seated Twists

Remaining in easy pose and bring your hands to the level of the shoulders at a 90-degree angle. Inhale and twist left; exhale and twist right. Breathe through your nose. Close your eyes and continue for 2-3 minutes.

This begins to deepen our work with the spine. This motion allows us to feel more limber in our spine and helps to send the energy upwards towards the crown.

4) Cat/Cow

Come onto all fours with your hands underneath the shoulders and hips in line with the knees. Keeping the arms straight, inhale and lift your heart and your tail (Cow). Exhale and round your back (Cat). Keep the breath moving through the nose. Close your eyes if you can and continue for 1-3 minutes.

This exercise is fabulous for posture and balance. It also stretches the spine, neck, hips, tummy, and back. It creates a beautiful emotional balance, relieves stress, and calms the mind.

5) Down Dog

Moving from cat/cow, exhale and lift your knees away from the floor. Lift the hips up towards the ceiling. Keep your fingers spread wide and your hands shoulder-width apart. Feet are hip-width apart, toes facing forward. Hips are pressed up and back, reaching the chest towards the thighs. Lift up through the tailbone to keep the spine straight and long. Let the neck and head hang freely from the shoulders, looking back between the knees or upper inner thighs.

Hold for 3-5 full breaths. This is possibly my favourite yoga pose as there is something about this pose that instantly connects me to the earth and to my heart.

On a physical level, it deeply stretches the back, opens the chest, and builds upper body strength. Using blocks underneath the hands or rolled up towels underneath the wrists will help with any initial discomfort.

6) Sun Salutation A (repeat the following series three times)

a.   Mountain Pose

* Stand straight with your feet a little apart and equal weight in each foot. Place your knee caps over the toes and gently firm the knee caps. Draw your tummy in and gently drop your tailbone. Hold your arms alongside the body with the palms open.

* Breathe deeply here, steadying the eyes and feeling into your body.

b.   Inhale and raise your arms up to the sky.

c.   Exhale and fold forward, keeping a soft bend in the knees and gently letting the head go.

d.   Bring your hands to your shins and come up into a halfway lift, pulling the belly in.

e.   Exhale and fold forward, placing the hands on the earth and stepping back into plank pose.

f.   Hold plank or come to the knees

g.   Slowly lower down to the earth.

h.   Inhale and lift up into cobra, keeping the pelvis connected to the earth and the elbows soft as you raise your heart to the sky.

i.   Exhale and surrender back down to the earth.

j.   Press into your hands. Come to your knees.

k.   Lift up and back into Downward Facing Dog, taking three deep breaths when you get there.

l.   Looking forward of your mat, step to the top of the mat and fold forward.

m.   Inhale halfway up and bring your hands to your shins.

n.   Exhale and fold back down.

o.   Press into your feet and ground into the earth as you inhale and take a reverse swan dive
        all the way up to the sky.

p.   Exhale the hands down to heart centre.

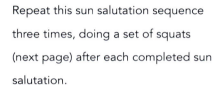

Repeat this sun salutation sequence
three times, doing a set of squats
(next page) after each completed sun
salutation.

7) Squats

Standing with your feet hip-width apart and arms reaching forward, take a breath in. Then, on the exhale, lower down into a squat, keeping the arms reaching forward. Inhale to rise up and lift the muscles of the pelvic floor. Exhale to lower and release the pelvic floor.

Stay focused on your breath. Fix your eyes on one point. Repeat 10 -15 squats (or more) after every sun salutation.

In yoga, when we lift up the muscles of the pelvic floor it is called Mula Bandha. There is so much power in this practice. On a physical level, it helps to engage our core muscles while lifting and aligning our entire body. On an energetic level, it helps to break our resistance to change, which lies within our root chakra. The more we practice it, the more we feel empowered energetically to make the right decisions for ourselves.

For women, we practice drawing up at the base of the pelvic floor and extending up to the mouth of the cervix. Draw in and up on the inhalation. Let go on the exhalation. Squats are literally magic for the root chakra. I practice them every day with Mula Bandha. They have the power to connect you to the earth element, bringing a sense of strength, grit, determination, and confidence.

8) Shaking

For 1- 5 minutes, turn on your favourite tribal music (I love and recommend A Tribe Called Red) and shake your body loose. Start with your left leg, lift it into the air and shake it in all different directions. Then repeat with the right leg, then the arms, then lift the shoulders up to the ears and then drop them down several times. Then just begin moving your body in different, organic ways.

Let yourself be free and move into an expression of whatever you need to rinse clean today. When we practice this in my classes, I ask my students to think of a past hurt or present-day stress that is a burden to them and to move it through the body by shaking it out. Remember that the body holds every emotion we don't know how to let go of. Shaking brings us the freedom to release our life force, let go of stagnant energy, and liberate every living cell.

9) Spinal Flush

Stand and reach your arms up to the sky as you breathe in. Exhale and fold forward, allowing the arms to let go, the head to release, and the body to surrender to the earth.

With every breath in, think "I am confident". With every breath out think, "I release fear". These energy classes are a blend of the physical and energetic. This fluid movement practice helps to clear old energy and bring in the new. Breathe in the state of being that you wish to feel and let the exhale release any resistance to stepping into that reality. Practice for 1- 3 minutes.

10) Happy Baby

This pose is not suitable if you are pregnant

Lying on the ground, grab the inner or outer edges of the feet and gently pull the knees down to the armpits. Position your knees over your ankles. Breathe in and out. Gently rock the body side to side and allow your hips to slowly open.

This pose is wonderful for relieving lower back pain and opening the hips, inner thighs, and the groin. It helps to calm a restless mind.

11) Legs Up the Wall

Another class favourite and my go-to pose if I need a gentle recharge. This pose is grounding, calming, and very nourishing. This pose is as simple as it looks; just lift your legs up and have your glutes as close as you can to the wall.

For the utmost benefits of this pose, practice for 5-10 minutes. This will relieve tired leg muscles, reduce edema in the legs and feet, and calm the nervous system.

12) Sweet Savasana

Ahh, the sweetest finish to any energetic practice; complete rest.

Savasana is the time when we are able to reap all of the benefits of our physical practice. Here, we relax into the earth and let her support us as we let go of any leftover tension we might still be experiencing.

This is the time when we channel energy inward to restore and revitalize our body and mind. Give yourself at least five minutes of rest on the earth. Support yourself in whatever way feels best to you. Let your breath become soft, let your eyes relax deep into the sockets, allow your tongue to rest on the lower pallet and begin to let go.

If you have trouble quieting your mind, one of the ways you can support yourself in this pose is through a simple mantra. With every inhale breathe in the words, whether repeating them softly out loud or allowing them to silently enter your mind, "I am confident," or "I am peaceful," or "I am courageous;" whatever rings the truest for you on this day. With every exhale, mentally or verbally repeat the words, "I let go".

Repeat repeat repeat…

Stay in savasana for at least 5 minutes. Stay connected to your heart. Feel your breath and breathe into your spirit.

13) Thymus Thump

When you have finished your rest pose, come to a comfortable seated position. Gently make a fist with your hand and lightly tap at the centre of the chest. Close your eyes and continue to breathe in and out. This simple exercise raises your life energy. The thymus gland's role is to keep your own life energy vibrating at a high frequency. When it is in balance, we feel stronger and more connected to who we really are. This is one of my favourite energetic exercises. When I need a quick boost, or a few minutes to reconnect to myself, I often practice this.

Adding a mantra while thumping at the thymus also increases your vibration. "I am confident, courageous, and filled with joy," is a great one.

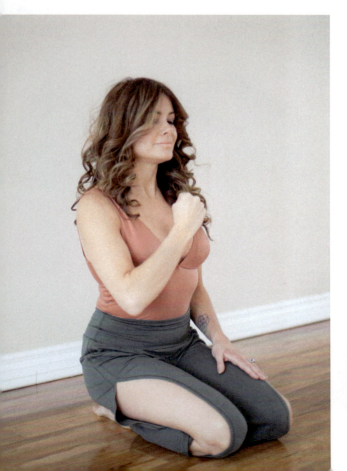

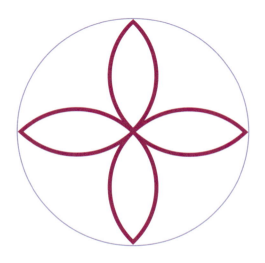

Energy Class for the Sacral & Solar Plexus Chakras

1) Connecting Pose

Now is the time to come into yourself. Sit comfortably and feel your spine nice and straight. Close your eyes and begin to take deep breaths in through the nose and out through the mouth. Release anything that you brought to your mat with ease and forgiveness. Move into the areas of the body that feel tight and restricted. Use your exhale to bring gentleness and release to these areas.

You may take your first finger and thumb together for Gyan Mudra. This mudra (aka hand gesture) creates balance, concentration, ease, and peace in the body, mind, and spirit. Breathe for a few minutes, holding this mudra and connecting to your centre.

When you feel ready, open your eyes to begin your practice.

All that matters right now is you...
Let the rest of the world go...

2) Pelvic Tilts

I love these. These tiny motions strengthen your low back and abdominal muscles.

Lie on your back with your knees bent and feet flat on the earth, close to your glutes. Exhale and engage your abdominal muscles, pulling your belly button down towards your spine. Feel the abs press the lower spine into the floor.

Inhale and press through your feet, allowing the tailbone to begin to curl up towards the ceiling. The hips, lower spine, and middle spine rise up. The legs stay parallel all the way through. Do not over-arch beyond your natural limit.

Exhale and use your abdominal control to roll the spine back down to the floor, vertebrae by vertebrae, as slowly as possible.

Repeat the exercise 3-5 times. This exercise is great for low back relief and helps open and stimulate the creativity of the sacral chakra.

3) Leg Lifts

This is one of the simplestest ways to begin creating a fire in your belly.

- Lie on your back, supporting yourself if needed by placing your hands underneath the sacrum with your thumbs touching.
- Lift the right leg up to the sky on an inhale and exhale as you return the leg fully to the earth.
- Lift the left leg up to the sky on the next inhale and exhale as you return the leg fully to the earth.
- Continue this motion for 1-3 minutes, moving with your breath.

This exercise will create abdominal strength and enhance your solar plexus chakra.

4) Legs to the Sky with Breath of Fire

Breath of Fire should not be practiced if you suffer from vertigo, high blood pressure, or a respiratory infection. If you are on your moon cycle, please use long, deep breaths instead.

Lifting the legs up to the sky with your hips on the floor, begin Breath of Fire.

Breath of Fire is also known as Kapalabhati Breath in Kundalini Yoga. It is one of my preferred breath practices in yoga because it holds so much transformative power. Breath of Fire will energize your entire body, clean the lungs and sinuses, and help you to build a lot of inner strength.

- Take a few deep breaths in and out to relax your body, mind, and spirit.
- Begin exhaling forcefully through your nose. As you are engaging this exhale, notice how your belly snaps back into your spine.
- Focus on your exhale and do not worry about the inhale; it will occur organically.
- Let the inhale be passive and the exhale be powerful.

Continue this practice for 1-2 minutes with your legs in the air.

In this photo my head is elevated. Please note that if this compromises your neck in any way, you should keep your head on the ground.

5) Bird of Strength

I named this exercise 'bird of strength' because this is how I feel when I practice it.
I literally feel as though I am going to take off into the sky!

- Lying on your back, use your core strength to draw the knees into your chest.
- Exhale and expand the legs out, keeping your abs engaged.
- Continue for 1-3 minutes, using your breath to fuel the motion.

Enjoy an inner strengthening and
a feeling of power as you take
flight with this exercise!

6) Floating Bridge Pose

This exercise is an amazing way to release energy from your body. It works really well after working on building heat in the area of the solar plexus.

- Set up for bridge pose by lying on your back with your feet close to your glutes. You should be able to tickle your ankles with your fingers.
- Reach your arms long overhead and rest them on the ground behind you. Interlace your fingers and release the first fingers with the left thumb placed over the right.
- Inhale and lift your hips to the sky and bring your arms up and over your head, reaching all the way to the thighs.

- Exhale and allow the arms to come back to first position over head while the torso, hips, and glutes melt back down to the earth.
- Continue this movement for 2-3 minutes, allowing the inhale and exhale to flow through the nose and fuel the motion.

7) Hip Circles

This practice will gently open your hips, bring you into focus, and connect you to the energy in your sacral chakra.

- Find a comfortable seated posture with one shin in front of the other.
- Move the torso in circles around the midline, inhaling as the body moves forward and exhaling as you move backwards.
- Practice these circles clockwise and then counterclockwise for up to three minutes on each side.

This movement will help to bring mobility to the hips and the spine. Hip circles also positively influence the adrenal glands and improve digestion.

8) Fluid Cat/Cow

This practice is the same set up as the traditional cat/cow that is described in the energy class for the Root Chakra. In the practice shown here, I am exploring moving my body differently. In these pictures I am reaching my hips back to my heels and then reaching up towards one side and then the other. You could liken it to big circles that the torso is exploring.

- Come onto all fours with your hands underneath the shoulders and hips in line with the knees.
- Send your hips back towards the heels. Start to round the torso up to the right side, then the left, then back towards the heels.
- Continue this motion in one direction for one minute, then switch the rotation and move in the opposite direction for another minute.

The magic of this practice is that it can become something different than what you see in these pictures and read in this description. Let yourself get lost in the motion, open your creativity, and allow your body to show you how it wants to move. The freedom of expression is magical and gives us confidence in ourselves.

9) Cat/Cow Reach

This practice helps to activate our core muscles and strengthen the energetic field around us.

- Come onto all fours with your hands underneath the shoulders and hips in line with your knees.
- Reach your right arm forward, allowing the shoulder to pull onto the back.
- Reach your left leg back, flexing your foot actively.
- Energize both your lifted arm and leg and create a firm base with your standing arm, engaged core, and the shin that's on the floor.
- Exhale and draw your lifted elbow to meet your knee at the midpoint of your body.
- Inhale and stretch the arm and leg away from each other.
- Continue for 1-2 minutes on one side, then switch and repeat with the other arm and leg.

This motion will help lengthen and stretch each side of your body while cultivating core strength and endurance. Move at an even pace, matching the inhale and exhale with your physical motion.

10) Down Dog to Wide Plank

This is a rhythmic motion to help stimulate your core, your hips, and your fluidity.

- Move organically from downward facing dog to plank pose.
- While in plank pose, stretch your hips back to your heels and widen your knees.
- Inhale as you come forward into plank pose.
- Exhale as you stretch the hips back to the heels, widening the knees.

Continue this motion for one minute. This practice increases your fluid nature and strengthens your core. This is a regular practice I include in all of my classes.

11) Child's Pose to Cobra

This is a continuous fluid motion that creates a surrender to the earth and an opening of the heart.

- From plank pose, send your knees to the earth, then drop the hips back to the heels in child's pose, keeping your arms stretched forward.
- Exhale in childs pose and lift your gaze forward, keeping your hands planted on the earth. Lift your forearms and torso and move up into cobra pose.
- Continue this motion back and forth, freeing the heart while surrendering to the earth for 1-3 minutes.

You will feel an elevation of your heart and a new connection to the earth in this practice.

12) Down Dog with Variation

Down dog can be a great exploratory posture. To me, it is a posture that allows us to say hello to our bodies. To take a deep breath and understand where we are stuck and where we might need more breath or space.

- Find the regular downward dog posture in your body (look to sequence one, Energy Class for the Root Chakra).
- Begin to bend one knee and stretch the opposite heel to the earth, switching legs with your breath.
- Bend both knees to the earth and lift your hips to the sky, breathing into the stretch of the body.
- Release the tension in your head and neck and breathe deeply, allowing your body to creatively express itself in this pose.

Experience this pose as long as you would like. Be mindful of your breath and allow yourself to flow into organic motion.

13) Big Circle

This is a motion that helps to open your energy field and create a feeling of expansion and strength.

- Stand with your feet wide apart and keep a soft bend in your knees.
- Interlace your hands above your head, straighten your arms, release the first fingers, and cross the left thumb over the right.
- Inhale in this position then exhale and let the arms lead the torso in big circles from one ankle to the other, circling up and around.
- Continue the motion in one direction for 1-2 minutes, then switch directions and repeat for an additional 1-2 minutes.

I love adding this motion into my classes. It is liberating and strengthening all at once. Try to close your eyes and let your breath guide you through this movement.

14) Shaking

Here it is again gals! The infamous shake out. This is an integral part of a daily practice. It doesn't require much effort; just turn on your favourite music and shake your body loose. Move your body in different ways, trying not to get caught up in one pattern of movement.

What is causing you stress in your life right now? What energy needs to leave your body? Bring intention into your movement. Breathe out what needs to leave and breathe in what you need more of in life.

Practice shaking for 1-5 minutes.

15) Spinal Flush

This practice is found in the Energy Class for the Root Chakra and is a full cleanse of your energy field.

- Standing, reach your arms up to the sky as you breathe in.
- Exhale and fold forward, allowing the arms to let go, the head to release, and the body to surrender to the earth.
- With every breath in think, "I am confident".
- With every breath out think, "I release fear".

Practice for 1-3 minutes.

These energy classes are a blend of the physical and energetic. This fluid movement practice helps to clear old energy and bring in the new. Breathe in the state of being that you wish to feel and let the exhale release any resistance to stepping into that reality.

16) Savasana

Sweet release.
Make your way onto your mat.

Savasana is the time when we are able to reap all of the benefits of our physical practice. Here, we relax into the earth and let her support us as we let go of any leftover tension we might still be experiencing.

This is the time when we channel energy inward to restore and revitalize our body and mind. Give yourself at least five minutes of rest on the earth. Support yourself in whatever way feels best to you. Let your breath become soft, let your eyes relax deep into the sockets, allow your tongue to rest on the lower pallet, and begin to let go.

Relax and surrender to the earth. Allow her to support you as you use your breath to take in the new and gently let go of the old.

As mentioned in the energy class for the root chakra, if it is difficult to let go of your mind, try bringing a powerful mantra into your awareness.

Breathe in, "I am enough".
Breathe out, "I let go".

Repeat, repeat, repeat.

Stay in savasana for at least 5 minutes. Stay connected to your heart, feel your breath, and breathe into your spirit.

17) Seated Posture

When it feels right for you, come to a seated position to close your practice. Align your spine, close your eyes, and soften your skin.

Breathe into all of the new space and energy in your body. Feel waves of gratitude and love move through you as you honor yourself and your commitment to you in this space and time.

Breathe in, "I am enough".
Breathe out, "I let go".

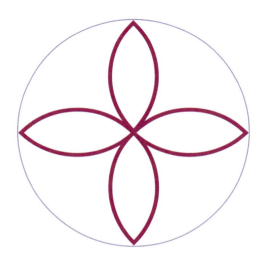

1) Connecting Pose

Come into a comfortable seated posture. Feel supported as you connect to the earth. Take the time to breathe. To experience your belly rise on the inhale and fall on the exhale. Connect to the energy in your body. What does it feel like today? Is there anything that needs to be released?

Use the next few minutes to bring your awareness to parts of your body that are holding energy and use your exhale to release them. When this feels complete, bring your hands into heart centre and press equally into the right and left palm.

Close your eyes.
Bring in an intention for your practice today.
When you feel ready, open your eyes and begin.

All that matters right now is you...
Let the rest of the world go...

2) Throat Tap

- Begin lightly tapping on your throat. Use your fingertips to stimulate and open the energy field of this area of the body.
- You may bring into your awareness the colour blue, which represents the throat chakra.
- Breathe in through the nose and out through the mouth.

Set the intention to open the energy channels of the heart and throat.

3) Dog Breath

- Staying in a comfortable seated posture, place your hands on your thighs and close your eyes.
- Begin breathing in and out through your mouth with your tongue sticking out of the mouth.
- On your last breath, inhale and hold your breath for 5-10 seconds while pressing the tongue against the upper palate.
- Exhale completely.
- Take a few moments to close your eyes and breathe normally into the openings that you have created through this practice.
- Feel how your energy has shifted and changed.
- Continue this sequence for up to three rounds, each round lasting 1-2 minutes.

This exercise opens the deep channels of the throat chakra. It helps to elevate stuck energy, freeing up space in the channel of the throat. It also brings energy to the immune system and helps the body fight infections. This is one of my favourites!

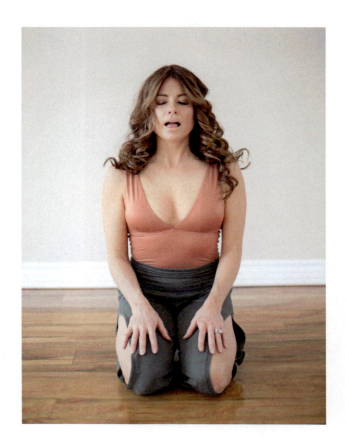

4) Shoulder Shrug

- Bring the shoulders up to the ears on an inhale and release them down the back with an exhale, breathing through the nose.
- Continue this exercise for 2-3 minutes.
- Take a few moments at the end of this practice to close your eyes and breathe into the space that has been created.

This exercise brings freedom to the tension we hold in our shoulders. I tell my students to imagine that all of the burdens they carry are being released with each exhale. You will notice a significant difference in the spaciousness around your shoulders and neck when you finish.

5) Neck Rolls

- Sit with a straight and relaxed spine.

- Begin to roll the neck slowly in one direction.

- Bring your breath into this exercise and allow the weight of the head to move the neck around.

- Breathe into all of the tight areas with awareness and the intention to let go of any stress.

- Do this for one minute, then change directions and repeat for another minute.

- Bring your head back to center, sit quietly, and connect with the sensations in your body and spine.

This exercise works on opening the throat chakra and opening the channels to the crown chakra. It also stimulates the thyroid.

6) Open and Close Arms

- Sit with a straight spine.
- Begin to open your arms wide and straight with an inhale and exhale as you bring the hands close together, but not touching.
- Continue to move rapidly, breathing in and out through your nose.
- Continue for 2-3 minutes.
- Sit and breath into your heart space. Feel the expansion of energy that has just been created.

This beautiful motion opens up the pathways of the heart chakra. It literally feels as though you are pumping up new energy from your heart. Close your eyes and allow yourself to connect to this motion. Imagine that green rays of heart energy are flowing out of the centre of your chest.

7) Cat/Cow

- Come onto all fours with your hands underneath your shoulders and hips in line with your knees.
- Keep the arms straight, inhale, and lift your heart and your tail (Cow). Exhale and round your back (Cat). Keep the breath moving through the nose.
- Close your eyes if you can and continue for 1-3 minutes.

This exercise is fabulous for posture and balance. It also stretches the spine, neck, hips, tummy, and back. It creates a beautiful emotional balance, relieves stress, and calms the mind.

8) Down Dog to Modified Chatarguna to Fluid Cobra

- Moving from cat/cow, exhale and lift your knees away from the floor. Lift the hips up towards the ceiling.
- Keep your fingers spread wide and your hands shoulder-width apart. Feet are hip-width apart, toes facing forward. Hips are pressed up and back, reaching the chest towards the thighs.
- Lift up through the tailbone to keep the spine straight and long. Let the neck and head hang freely from the shoulders, looking back between the knees or upper inner thighs.

Hold for 3-5 full breaths.

- Float forward into plank pose and hold for a full inhale and exhale.
- Let your knees come to the earth.
- Breathe in.

- Exhale and, slowly bending the elbows, lower yourself to the mat.
- Keep your hands connected to the earth underneath your shoulders and on your next inhalation begin to straighten the arms to lift the chest up off the floor, going only to the height at which you can maintain a connection between your pelvis and the earth.

- Breathe into your heart centre, then exhale and slowly descend back to the earth.

- This motion can turn into a fluid, moving cobra.
- Press into your right hand with a little bit more pressure and roll up the right shoulder, then press into the left hand and roll up the left shoulder.
- Repeat 3-6 times and let your body guide you with its own unique rhythm.

Cobra pose has the power to open your heart chakra. Imagine your heart is like a compass and it is lighting the way forward each time you rise up in this pose.

9) Fluid Back Bends

- Standing tall, interlace your hands at the centre of your chest, releasing the first finger and crossing the left thumb over the right.
- Inhale and stretch your arms long, engage your core, keep your biceps by your ears, and bend backward.
- Exhale and bring your back and arms to the starting position.

This motion opens the upper back and heart. Allow yourself to move with the intention of opening the heart. Move at your own pace and let your breath be your guide.

10) Sun Salutation A (repeat the following series three times)

a.   Mountain Pose

            * Stand straight with your feet a little apart and equal weight in each foot. Place your knee caps over the toes and gently firm the knee caps. Draw your tummy in and gently drop your tailbone. Hold your arms alongside the body with the palms open.

            * Breathe deeply here, steadying the eyes and feeling into your body.

b.   Inhale and raise your arms up to the sky.

c.   Exhale and fold forward, keeping a soft bend in the knees and gently letting the head go.

d.   Bring your hands to your shins and come up into a halfway lift, pulling the belly in.

e.   Exhale and fold forward, placing the hands on the earth and stepping back into plank pose.

f.   Hold plank or come to the knees

g.   Slowly lower down to the earth.

h.   Inhale and lift up into cobra, keeping the pelvis connected to the earth and the elbows soft as you raise your heart to the sky.

i.   Exhale and surrender back down to the earth.

j.   Press into your hands. Come to your knees.

k.   Lift up and back into Downward Facing Dog, taking three deep breaths when you get there.

l.   Looking forward of your mat, step to the top of the mat and fold forward.

m.   Inhale halfway up and bring your hands to your shins.

n.   Exhale and fold back down.

o.   Press into your feet and ground into the earth as you inhale and take a reverse swan dive all the way up to the sky.

p.   Exhale the hands down to heart centre.

Repeat this sun salutation sequence three times, doing a set of squats after each completed sun salutation.

11) Down Dog Lunges

- From downward facing dog, lift your right leg up to the sky, then exhale and step it forward to the inner right hand.
- Place the knee directly over the ankle. Tuck the back toes under and straighten the back leg.
- Keep the back leg in extension by pressing the back heel away from you and the back of the knee up to the ceiling. The modification, as shown, is dropping the back knee to the earth.
- Relax the hips, allowing them to sink towards the floor.
- Allow your arms to move into goal post position, squeezing the shoulder blades together and presenting the heart forward.
- Breathe into your heart space for 3-5 full breaths.
- Switch sides and repeat.

Heart-opening lunges are powerful. They help to stretch and open our legs and hips, while elevating the torso up to the sky. Breathe deeply here. Close your eyes and feel the earth energy support your roots as your heart reaches toward the sky.

12) Fish Pose

Skip this pose if you have high or low pressure or a low back or neck injury.

- Lie on your back with your legs stretched out and your arms resting beside your body. If you need added support in this pose, bring your hands to touch underneath your sacrum.
- Press your forearms and elbows into the earth and lift your chest to create an arch in your upper back. Lift your shoulder blades and upper torso off the floor.
- Gently allow your head to tilt back, bringing the crown of the head towards the floor. Keep your thighs active and energized. Do not allow much weight to rest on the crown of your head.
- Hold for five breaths. To release the pose, press firmly through your forearms to slightly lift your head off the floor. Exhale as you lower your torso and head to the floor.

Fish pose is amazing for opening the heart and the throat chakra. Let yourself soften as much as you can in the pose, using your breath to create an opening in these areas of the body.

13) Sat Nam

This powerful mantra is described in the opening pages of *The Confidence Project*. *Sat* means truth. *Nam* means name. Together they mean, "I am Truth," or "Truth is my essence".

The more you chant this mantra, the more you will feel connected to and living in your absolute truth.

- Sit back on the heels, supporting yourself with a block or pillow if needed.
- Interlace your hands above your head, releasing the first finger and crossing the left thumb over the right.
- Inhale and mentally think or chant out loud, "*Sat*".
- Exhale and mentally think or chant out loud, "*Nam*".
- On the inhale, draw the belly in. On the exhale, gently let it go.
- Continue this for 3-5 minutes.

Close your eyes and be with this powerful mantra. Allow it to permeate your energy field. Commit to its resonance and truth in your being. It will transform you, helping you to clearly see the powerful, amazing being you are!

14) Savasana

Sweet Rest.

Find the most comfortable position you can on your mat.

Savasana is the time when we are able to reap all of the benefits of our physical practice. Here we relax into the earth and let her support us as we let go of any leftover tension we might still be experiencing.

This is the time when we channel energy inward to restore and revitalize our body and mind. Give yourself at least five minutes of rest on the earth. Support yourself in whatever way feels best to you. Let your breath become soft, let your eyes relax deep into the sockets, allow your tongue to rest on the lower pallet and begin to let go.

Breathe in the words, "I am courageous".
Breathe out the words, "I let go".

Breathe in, "I am worthy of all good things in my life".
Breathe out, "I let go".

Breathe in, "I am filled with self love".
Breathe out, "I let go".

Stay in savasana for at least 5 minutes. Stay connected to your heart, feel your breath, and breathe into your spirit.

In addition to this journal, I'm excited to share with you *The Confidence Project Online Program*. This online course is designed to empower you to live your best life. If you found insight through the exercises in this journal, you can take it one step further by exploring the classes offered online.

The online program is full of guided yoga flows and meditations to help you take your journey to confidence to the next level. In addition, by joining the course you'll receive a playlist full of relaxing and meditative music perfect for playing in the background as you work your way through the reflective prompts in this journal.

Whether you choose to follow the entire course as I guide you back to your highest self or simply visit a class or a meditation that speaks to you when you feel in need of a boost, this course will be there for you throughout your journey to confidence.

Learn more at www.CarolBaxter.ca/TheConfidenceProject and use the code TCPJOURNAL10 when signing up to save 10% off the full price of the course.